USING TECHNOLOGY TO INCREASE STUDENT LEARNING

To the staff, parents, and students of Walt Disney School . . .
I'm proud to work with you!

USING TECHNOLOGY TO INCREASE STUDENT LEARNING

LINDA E. REKSTEN

CORWIN PRESS, INC.
A Sage Publications Company
Thousand Oaks, California

For information:

Corwin Press, Inc.
A Sage Publications Company
2455 Teller Road
Thousand Oaks, California 91320
E-mail: order@corwinpress.com

Sage Publications Ltd.
6 Bonhill Street
London EC2A 4PU
United Kingdom

Sage Publications India Pvt. Ltd.
M-32 Market
Greater Kailash I
New Delhi 110 048 India

Printed in the United States of America

Library of Congress Cataloging-in-Publication Data

Reksten, Linda E.
    Using technology to increase student learning/by Linda E. Reksten.
        p. cm.
Includes bibliographical references.
    ISBN 0-8039-6813-2 (cloth: alk. paper)
    ISBN 0-8039-6814-0 (pbk.: alk paper)
    1. Educational technology—United States. 2. Education.
    Elementary—United States—Computer-assisted instruction. 3.
    Instructional systems—United States—Design. I. Title.
        LB1028.3.R44 2000
        371.33—dc21   99-050607

This book is printed on acid-free paper.

00 01 02 03 04 05 10 9 8 7 6 5 4 3 2 1

Corwin Editorial Assistant: Catherine Kantor
Production Editor: Denise Santoyo
Editorial Assistant: Nevair Kabakian
Typesetter: Danielle Dillahunt
Designer: Tina Hill
Cover Designer: Michelle Lee

Contents

Preface

....

With the mounting stress to implement the continuous flow of educational reforms such as technology, school principals are overwhelmed with the challenge of making these changes in their schools. This book was developed to provide a practical pathway to building an effective technology program at a school site. There is no question that technology is at the forefront of school reform by policymakers at every level of government. The ambitious Federal "E-rate" telecommunications services program intends that every school and library will be connected to the Internet by the 21st century. In addition, technology expertise is considered mandatory by business leaders for students entering the workplace. Opinion polls indicate that parents feel that technology is critical to a child's education.

Educational leaders do not deny the need for technological proficiency by students, as shown by the millions spent on school technologies by state Departments of Education and private enterprise. Both policymakers and the public, however, are starting to demand hard evidence that these investments in educational technology have been worthwhile in improving student performance as shown in test scores.

Along with these "external" policy issues, there is the additional pressure on principals to provide the necessary "internal" leadership and support for implementing technology innovation with school staffs that may be resistant to the radical change that technology will bring. This book addresses the kind of responsive leadership necessary to bring about the change technology will demand. Unfortunately, most change is implemented from traditional top-down, coercive bureaucratic structures and will achieve minimal change and minimal results.

From an extensive body of effective schools research regarding the introduction of innovations such as technology, it is known that the leadership and response behaviors of principals are linked to the development of a collaborative workplace so necessary to managing the kind of change technology will demand (Reksten, 1995; Rosenholtz, 1989). There is further evidence by Little (1982) that a collaborative workplace spawns innovative practice such as technology and risk taking by teachers. Responsive leadership will encourage the kind of risk taking that will achieve greater results.

Another viewpoint that links to student achievement, often overlooked with technology implementation, is that technology is designed to be a "tool" in the hands of educators and students and to be vitally linked with the curriculum. Often technology is viewed as a curriculum unto itself rather than a curricular tool much the same as paper and pencils are tools in the hands of students. Consequently, much of technology in schools today consists of students participating in closed-ended tutorial programs in reading and math rather than open-ended approaches using technology to construct meaning with curriculum projects, which can ultimately lead to the kind of student outcomes we are looking for from this investment.

Practitioners need to know and understand that for technology to be used as a tool, three foundational elements must be in place, and they must know how to create these elements. First, the school climate or context of a school, addressed in Chapters 1 and 2, must allow for the kind of necessary changes that teachers and students will need to make. A coercive "boss" system of management, so common to the organizational structures of education, will not encourage teachers to take risks and make the kind of dramatic changes that using technology with students demands. Ordering staff to make changes will gain only minimal effort from staff—since making mistakes is often viewed by administration as incompetence. Instead, there must be a "lead management" (Glasser, 1990) structure in place where the principal leads the school team through change by encouragement and example. In this structure, there is freedom to take risks and make mistakes. Staff collaboration and risk taking in this structure are viewed as a means of learning and growing toward achieving the goals for students.

Along with a positive school context, the curriculum must be organized through concept-based instruction for effective technology integration. This issue is addressed in Chapter 3. Because the curriculum is organized by concepts, learning activities become integrated, as they are in life, so that students use skills and processes for constructing meaning and solving problems. Because the use of technology is integrated by nature, in that any use of a computer involves multiple tasks, technology becomes a perfect fit for concept-based instruction.

In addition, the use of concept-based instruction does not compromise the teaching of basic skills. Instead it extends those basic skills to meaningful applications that encourage thinking and independent learning, again paralleling the demands of the workplace. Also, through organizing the curriculum into concepts, essential understandings, and guided questions, students are exposed to ever-deepening levels of understanding the

"Big Ideas." Students therefore increasingly develop critical integrated process skills, which link directly to their student achievement. Linking concepts through grade-level articulation helps to maintain the consistency of critical understandings taught at grade levels. With curriculum organized in this manner, a school can take full advantage of technology tools.

A workable action plan discussed in Chapter 4 is the third foundational component of successfully integrating technology. This technology plan must not be cumbersome. It must be practical and allowed to evolve according to the needs of the school site. A technology plan should be a living document, not one that is buried on a shelf after it has been formulated, which is often the case in most schools. Thus, an effective plan must outline the beginning action steps a school staff is committed to taking in effecting technology change. These steps are intimately linked with a focused curriculum and the leadership structure of the school.

An effective technology plan should first and foremost address the student processes and skills that are transferable and that will develop independent learning. These skills are intimately connected to student expectancies. What we want students to achieve must drive everything we do in technology. How curriculum is linked with technology skills is the second most important part of a technology plan and addressed in Chapter 5. Chapter 7 addresses the use of the Internet to enrich and enhance curriculum and instruction as well as to provide students with opportunities to create Web sites or showcase their curriculum projects.

These curricular connections require collaborative planning and communication. From student expectancies and a focused curriculum developed by staff, decisions regarding hardware and software can be made. These important decisions are discussed in Chapter 6. Based on what hardware and software tools are acquired, staff will need to be trained in the use of these tools with curriculum and the management of the technology environment. Five models of collaborative staff training are discussed in Chapter 8.

Maintaining a technology environment whereby the greatest access for students can be ensured is a daunting task. Computers and the wiring that connects them always experience problems. The technology environment as discussed in Chapter 9 addresses the changes and challenges that can potentially encourage or discourage staff, depending upon the management structure of the school. If computer equipment is consistently under repair or faulty for long periods of time, teachers will stop implementing the technology program.

As these essential elements of a technology plan are implemented, staff will consistently develop new technology skills and expertise that will result in student growth and application of process skills so necessary for future employment.

This book and the story behind it would not have been possible without the help of many people. Above all, I am grateful to Dr. JoAnn Ratcliff, my editor, who carefully guided me through a difficult doctoral dissertation process and helped me to write this text with clarity and "passion." Also, I am indebted to Joni Olmstead, graphic artist and good friend, who has spent countless hours with me preparing the student figures and illustrations. I am also grateful to the outstanding teachers at Walt Disney School whom I have had the privilege of working with for 13 years. They are truly a collaborative and innovative team that has made our school not only a California Distinguished School but a model technology school. Finally, I am tremendously proud of my students at Walt Disney School who will someday "be somebody" and positively influence our world.

About the Author

....

Linda E. Reksten has been an educator in the public schools for 17 years. A native of Montana, she graduated from Montana State University, Billings in 1973 with a Secondary Education degree in biology and chemistry. Immediately after graduating, she went on to earn a Master's degree in Christian education from George Fox University in 1976 and served 4 years as a Director of Christian Education.

She began her public teaching career in the Burbank Unified School District in 1980 as a middle school science teacher and high school chemistry teacher. During the summers, she taught elementary science for gifted students in grades 4 and 5. While still a teacher, she began her second Master's degree at Point Loma Nazarene College where she graduated in curriculum and administration during the summer of 1985. During 1986, she became principal of Walt Disney Elementary School. Within one year, she began her doctoral studies at UCLA in Teaching Studies and completed them in June 1995, while she was a principal.

Throughout her 13 years as principal, Walt Disney School has become a Title 1 school and the most ethnically diverse school in Burbank, with 12 languages and 50% of the student population speaking only limited English. In spite of these challenges, Walt Disney School became a model technology school in Los Angeles County and a California Distinguished School during May 1997. She also completed a video series for National School Conference Institute (NSCI) during 1998 and 1999, which has been aired to subscribing schools across the country. She has also presented workshops at the NSCI Conference, "Building the 21st Century Elementary School" in San Diego, California and Phoenix, Arizona, and will be presenting for NSCI during the 1999/2000 school year.

CHAPTER 1

The Challenge of Building a Quality Technology Program

....

Educational practitioners, superintendents, directors of curriculum, coordinators, and especially site principals are being pressured to develop "quality" technology programs in their schools. There is no question that technology is at the forefront of school reform advocated by policymakers at every level of government. Business leaders consider technology expertise to be mandatory preparation for the workplace. This is especially true of the new School-to-Work emphasis energized by Willard Daggett, J. D. Hoye, and others. Furthermore, opinion polls also indicate that parents feel that technology is as basic as reading, writing, and arithmetic to their child's education.

Certainly, most educational leaders do not deny the need for technological proficiency by students—witness the increase in the amount of money spent on technologies by state Departments of Education over the past 3 years. However, policymakers and the public are now starting to demand evidence from schools that their investments in educational technology are worth the money. There is a rising concern that spending large amounts of money on technology will not guarantee improved student achievement or even assist reform efforts. Even now, lawmakers are considering cutting or dismantling the federal "E-rate" discount program for telecommunications services to schools and libraries that adds networking infrastructure for Internet access.

In the face of all the criticisms and skepticism of policymakers, how can schools develop a "quality" technology program, improve their students' achievement, and quell the fears of critics? I believe we can create quality technology programs given that we confront head on what we need to do to lay the groundwork for the change technology requires. We need systematically to create the school environment that will permit technology's positive and dramatic impact on student learning to occur and flourish. Four critical elements are requisite: the principal's leadership, the view of curriculum, the role of technology in curriculum, and a workable plan. Each is in the hands and heart of the principal. This book provides principals with a practical pathway for creating the right environment and implementing technology at their school site to improve student achievement. It also offers school principals and leadership teams guidance and action steps without the technical jargon that could frustrate any reasonable effort to implement technology.

The Technology Research

Research conducted so far on the effectiveness of technology in the classroom reports mixed findings. Some evidence exists that basic skills can be improved through drill and practice with computer programs, but there are few definitive measures for more sophisticated uses of technology in the classroom. There is also a mismatch between the kinds of changes that technology is expected to produce and the kinds of outcome measures used to show results.

Harold Wenglinsky (1998), in a groundbreaking study on the effectiveness of technology with fourth and eighth graders, showed that computers can raise student achievement and even improve a school's climate. However, Wenglinsky says that computers have to be placed in the right hands and used in the right ways. If used for the wrong purposes, computers appear to do more harm than good. Wenglinsky analyzed student math achievement from the 1996 National Assessment of Educational Progress (NAEP) Study. He found that students whose teachers used computers mainly for math applications rather than for drill and practice scored higher than students whose teachers didn't. In both the fourth and eighth grades, students whose teachers had professional development in technology outperformed students whose teachers did not (Wenglinsky, 1998).

With this new research by Wenglinsky and the extensive body of effective schools research, which is known to support the introduction of a new innovation such as technology, principals must think in terms of preparing their staffs for changes that are surely coming. This preparation involves identifying the critical elements of building a successful technology program that will result in the student's achievement.

The principal's leadership is the first critical element; it is well known that leadership and response behaviors of principals have been linked to the development of the collaborative workplace that is so essential to the introduction of change (Reksten, 1995; Rosenholtz, 1989). There is further evidence, by Judith Little (1982), that a collaborative workplace spawns innovative practices such as technology as well as risk taking by teachers. Without a leadership style that is supportive of the change that is expected of teachers to improve student achievement, the innovation will probably fail. There is a big difference between being a leader and being a "boss." Only a leader who has a clear vision of student improvement targets and is committed to working shoulder to shoulder with staff to reach these targets can mobilize staff to make changes. This kind of leadership will most often create a collaborative work environment that will ultimately lead to consistent, innovative instructional practice.

How curriculum is viewed within the school is the second critical element. The way curriculum is organized and implemented is essential to the kind of outcomes we want for students. The best way to encourage student thinking and learning is to organize curriculum by concepts rather than by just facts. Curriculum that is integrated and concept based encourages students to apply knowledge to real-life situations. A curriculum that is fact based will rarely promote high levels of achievement by students.

A principal's perception of technology with curriculum is the third critical element. If technology is viewed as separate from curriculum or as a distinct curriculum, it will never be used to encourage student achievement. Instead, technology will be used as a tutorial for drill and practice with the curriculum defined by that software program. These software programs may or may not support the grade-level curriculum standards. Technology must instead be used as a tool augmenting concept-based instruction and curriculum that, in turn, originates from the classroom teacher. Because technology skills are themselves already integrated, students are immediately required to use thinking skills to produce a product. Integrating technology skills with a concept-based curriculum results in a powerful combination to improve student thinking as well as student achievement.

Developing a workable plan is the fourth critical element. This plan must communicate the commitment your staff has to technology. A plan is essentially an oath consisting of what everyone promises to do and a description of the action steps. The best plans are those that are so well communicated that they "live" within the minds of your staff. These plans are dynamic and ever-evolving as your staff grows in technology expertise. Technology plans will need yearly revision to reflect the growth and many changes that will take place.

These critical elements will determine the kind of technology program at your school and, more important, whether the investment made in technology will result in the student achievement you want to see.

Leadership Comes First

In order for technology change or any innovative change to take place in schools, I believe we need a new paradigm for leadership. The most common and widely held view of leadership in education is that of a *manager or boss*. The emphasis in this type of leadership is on making sound decisions, creating sensible policies, and allocating rewards or penalties based on formal assessments of individual contributions to organizational goals. For any complex change to occur in schools, or even for schools to keep pace with change in society, there is a need to break out of the traditional pattern of "boss" management.

The traditional manager or boss operates at all levels of education. Teachers are in charge of students. Principals are in charge of teachers. District officers are in charge of principals. The Superintendent is charge of all District personnel. The Board of Education is in charge of the Superintendent and District. The State Board of Education is in charge of the State and so on. The very nature of the terms *manager* and *boss* means to be "in charge of." However, merely being in charge of either students or teachers does not make a manager a leader or even a good manager.

The traditional structure of what Glasser (1990) terms "boss" management is based on Skinner's stimulus response theory. In Skinner's famous experiment, food rewards were given to mice to elicit certain desirable behaviors. Punishments by electric shock were also administered to mice, forcing them through fear to perform certain behaviors. Current educational management has applied Skinner's theories by motivating educators to do their best work through giving extrinsic rewards (financial incentives) or punishments (competency exams) to achieve goals. Research by Lortie (1975) and others, however, has shown that extrinsic incentives are not effective motivators for improving teacher performance. In addition, forcing teachers to comply with boss management through punitive measures results in only minimal performance and low-quality work, as the worker does "only what is necessary to get by." As a result, the organization never produces quality work.

Glasser (1990), in *The Quality School*, described the objectives of a "boss" management structure so prevalent in education:

- *The boss determines the task and the standards for what teachers are to do, without consulting the teachers.* There is no compromise, and the teachers simply have to adjust to the boss's demands.

- *The boss usually tells, rather than shows, the teachers how the work is to be done.* The boss rarely asks teachers how the work could be done better.

- *The boss inspects or grades the work.* Since the teachers are not involved in the evaluation, the teachers do just enough work to get by.

- *When workers resist, the boss uses coercion or punishment to make teachers do as they are told.* This creates a workplace where the boss and the teachers are adversaries. (pp. 25-26)

From these objectives it is clear that boss management is more concerned with the needs of the boss and organizational goals than with the workers. This structure "fits" education where teachers and administrators tend to want to control those of whom they are in charge. A good student is one who is "doing what he [or she] is told." For example, good student discipline policies are ones that "get tough with students" and force them to comply.

This traditional management structure has led to a culture of boss management in education where administrators and teachers rarely question decisions made from the top. Districts are often run like a factory—top down, coercive, rigid, and calculating, designed to stifle creativity and independent judgment as well as maintain control over the workers. Boss management has been shown to be outdated, archaic, and ineffective at all levels, and it is particularly harmful at higher levels of leadership. A principal who is a dedicated boss-manager will prevent those whom he or she supervises from producing quality work and will negatively affect the entire school (Glasser, 1990, p. 30). The sad news is that educators are not even aware that better management structures exist.

Bringing Staff to Collaboration

In contrast to coercive boss management, according to Glasser (1990), Lead Management is what schools need. The Leader Manager uses persuasion and problem-solving and spends his or her time trying to improve the school so that workers will want to do quality work. A leader manager is responsible for establishing purpose and direction for teachers so that teachers will want to commit to quality education for students.

When lead management principles are put into place at schools, teachers come to believe that the principal is as concerned with their needs as they are. This does not mean that principals should not address teachers who fail to put effort into their responsibilities of teaching. On the contrary, principals must be open and honest with teachers and work with them to solve their problems. Using technology is fraught with problems, and the principal must help teachers navigate through them.

Collaboration requires a positive school context. There is little doubt that the leadership of the principal is linked to the school context. In my research, I found that certain context variables had an impact on improved teacher performance: Collaboration, Innovation, Principal Leadership, Principal Response, and School Community. Of these, innovation and principal response were viewed as most important by high-performing teachers. Principal leadership, which was defined as setting goals, setting priorities, and providing a strong direction for the school, showed a weak but significant relationship to a teacher's sense of personal competency. Although teachers felt these activities were important for a principal to carry out, principal responsiveness was noted as even more important. Consequently, a principal who is perceived by teachers as separate from and unresponsive to them, even though the principal provides direction and leadership, was not as significant as a principal who was responsive to the needs of staff. Principal leadership alone does not sufficiently address the needs of teachers, who very often are isolated and uncertain about their practice (Rosenholtz, 1989). However, when principal leadership and principal response are combined, as in the lead management model, teachers can be developed into an effective collaborative school team (Reksten, 1995). With this research in mind, principals must realize that leadership is a combination of leading, managing, and responding to staff over time in order to develop a positive, collaborative school context. It is from this investment of time and energy that a "quality" program will emerge.

Technology Equals Innovation

The context variable innovation was identified by teachers as the most significant of the five context variables assessed (Reksten, 1995). What proved to be even more interesting was that teachers felt that collaboration was fundamental to generating innovative practices. Collaboration—such as planning together, peer coaching, and sharing about the teaching practice—that is continuous and consistent sets up "habits" of collegial working. These habits provide teachers a forum for sharing ideas and a support base from which it becomes safe to try these new ideas. In addition, a confidence develops when new skills are tried without fear of punishment. In this kind of school context, teachers are free to launch into technology change (Reksten, 1995). A collaborative school context will provide the support structure for technology change not only to occur but to be maintained.

The View of Technology and Curriculum

Along with preparing a collaborative workplace, how principals view technology's integration with curriculum is vitally important. Administrators must realize that technology is a "tool" in the hands of educators and students, much the same as paper and pencils. Often technology is viewed as a curriculum unto itself, separate and apart from the regular curriculum. Much of technology in schools today consists of students participating in closed-ended tutorial programs in reading and math rather than in open-ended approaches using technology that allows students to construct meaning with curriculum projects, which can ultimately lead to the kind of student outcomes that we are looking for from this investment.

Practitioners need to know and understand that for technology to be used as a tool, the curriculum must be organized around concept-based instruction, ready for effective technology integration. When the curriculum is organized by concepts, learning activities are integrated, as they are in life, so that students use skills and processes for constructing meaning and solving problems. Because the use of technology is integrated by nature, in that any use of a computer involves multiple tasks, technology is a perfect fit for concept-based instruction.

The use of concept-based instruction also does not compromise the teaching of basic skills. Instead it extends those basic skills to meaningful applications that encourage thinking and independent learning, again paralleling the demands of the workplace. Also, through organizing curriculum into essential understandings and guided questions, students increasingly develop critical integrated processes and skills that link directly to their student achievement. Linking these concepts through grade-level articulation (e.g., curriculum mapping) helps to maintain the consistency of critical understandings taught at grade levels. With an integrated curriculum organized in this manner, a school can take full advantage of technology tools.

In preparing a staff for the kind of change that technology will demand, principals and school leadership teams will need to ask themselves the following:

- "What is our view of leadership for technology?"
- "What is needed at our school to create a collaborative workplace?"
- "What is our view of curriculum?"
- "What is our view of how technology integrates with the curriculum?"

The answers to these questions will determine how technology will be used in your program and, ultimately, whether improved student achievement will occur.

Developing a Workable Plan

A workable action plan is vital to integrating technology successfully. This technology plan must not be cumbersome; it must be practical and allowed to evolve according to the needs of a school site. A technology plan should be a living document, not one that is buried on a shelf after it has been formulated, which is often the case in the field today. An effective plan must outline the beginning action steps a school staff is committed to taking in effecting technology change. These steps are intimately linked with a focused curriculum and a supportive lead management structure in the school.

An effective technology plan should first and foremost address student expectancies and outcomes. What we want students to achieve must drive everything we do in using technology. How curriculum is linked with technology skills is the second most important part of a technology plan. This connection requires collaborative planning and communication. From student expectancies and a focused curriculum developed by staff, good decisions regarding the acquisitions of hardware and software tools can be made. Based on what tools are acquired, staff training will need to be structured, as well as an ongoing management system that ensures the greatest access for students. Management of technology changes every day; new and challenging developments can potentially encourage or discourage staff, depending on the management structure of the school. In addition, as these essential elements of a plan are implemented, staff will be constantly evaluating and changing as new skills and expertise develop. This could be potentially threatening if the climate of the school is a negative one.

Pressure on schools to verify that technology spending can make a difference in student achievement is increasing, and your school can prepare for changes that are needed. Foundational to any change is the kind of leadership you or your leadership team exercises at your school. The coercive boss management style will never lead to a quality program. Responsive lead management is needed to develop the kind of collaborative support structure that will fuel the many changes that technology will demand. When an inviting school context is present at your school, norms of collegiality will be established. As a result, teachers will be welded into an effective school team willing to work with one another and take technology risks.

A principal's view of technology in relation to the curriculum is critical to how it will be implemented. Technology is not a curriculum, but a tool for curriculum. Focusing and organizing the curriculum by concepts provides the basis for technology to be used. Concept-based teaching, along with technology tools, will elevate student thinking and improve achievement overall. This kind of organization will target your curriculum toward improving student achievement.

Finally, developing a workable plan is another important step in the preparation for change. The achieving of student expectancies must be the focus of any technology plan. This plan should be a simple set of action steps that guide the implementation of technology. These action steps should address curriculum, hardware and software tools, staff training, and ongoing management during implementation. By addressing these three areas of change, your school will eliminate some of the common pitfalls along the road of technology.

Creating a School Context for Technology Change

....

The introduction of technology always brings tremendous change and risk to a teaching staff. Even with adequate training, many teachers find technology threatening, at the very least. This is especially the case for teachers who are resistant to change, who fear failing at something new, or who are overwhelmed by the responsibilities of teaching. These teachers tend to avoid situations in which they doubt their ability to perform successfully (Ashton & Webb, 1986). For example, teachers who are mandated to use computers with instruction often give up or ignore using them with students because it is too difficult or requires too much time and energy. Very often schools and districts ignore such responses from teachers and "march" ahead with a technology program imposed by a top-down, coercive management that fails to lead its teachers to some level of comfort or confidence in using technology (Dembo & Gibson, 1985). Ignoring these teacher issues usually results in resistance and may well end or curtail a school's use of technology before it really has a chance to begin. These teachers are a part of your school context, along with other staff, community members, parents, and students. The critical prerequisite for successful technology integration is preparing your staff and your school community to take on the positive aspects of an inviting school "context" for technology change.

The School Context

Preparing a school context for change is a difficult task for even the best of principals and leadership teams. It is imperative, however, that leadership provide a place where people enjoy working. This is especially true in regard to the changes that education is now requiring and will continue to require (Fullan, 1982). Effective schools research on school context and change has been very helpful to me as a practicing principal and has shaped the direction of my thinking for creating that "inviting context" (Martin, 1990).

I believe there is a convincing amount of effective schools research by Rosenholtz (1985, 1986, 1987, 1989) and others indicating that the school context can influence a teacher's sense of personal empowerment and thereby influence student learning. By definition, the school context is a community consisting of the students, teachers, classified staff, parents, and administrators working as a collaborative team both organizationally and interpersonally. The school context must be positive for integrated technology first to occur and second to flourish. I've found that it is invariably true that a positive context encourages staff commitment to a strong academic emphasis, high expectations of students, clear incentive and reward systems, continual monitoring of student work, and providing students with corrective feedback (Newmann, Rutter, & Smith, 1989). In order for your school to reflect this kind of positive context for student achievement, you must begin with teachers and, more important, with your own administrative leadership. Administration must be willing to "roll up its sleeves" and literally be the very model of a collaborative work process so that teachers collectively can be trained, then empowered to deliver effective instruction to students.

In contrast, a negative school context is characterized by an absence of collaborative teamwork; that is, a distinct separation between teachers and administration. Teachers in this context are often isolated and "live out" a separate existence. Both Lortie (1975) in *School Teacher* and Goodlad (1984) in *A Place Called School* point to teacher isolation as a major factor that clearly impacts school effectiveness. An effect of isolation is the development of individualistic viewpoints rather than collective beliefs about helping students learn or how success should be measured (Tye & Tye, 1983). Isolated teachers become very narrow-minded, and effectiveness tends to be measured by a teacher's personal beliefs about what should be learned rather than an integrative effort of schoolwide coordination. You can count on the fact that, in most instances, isolated teachers—except for "techies"—will resist technology per se and resist the integration of technology into the curriculum.

Bringing about a positive collaborative context is not easy and it requires time. In my own experience, it required 5 years of consistently implementing three vital elements. *Responsive leadership* that listens and follows through with staff is paramount as the first vital element. Collaboration begins with the principal's responsiveness. Teachers must come to believe that principals will listen and act on their needs.

Taken together, *habits of collegial working* that are not only structured by the principal but led by the principal, constitute the second vital element in building a positive school context. It is not enough for a principal to schedule time for teachers to reflect, analyze, and evaluate their instruction or student work, the process must be led and modeled by the principal. Teachers must see that the principal is not afraid to get his or her hands dirty with them in the grueling work of education. This habitual modeling and interaction of the principal with teachers welds teachers into collaborative teams. Teachers working with the principal begin to see themselves in a new light. They become excited about trying new ideas and sharing leadership roles.

From responsive leadership, collaborative teams develop a common mission—to improve student achievement. Collaboration produces a collective belief system among teachers about their role in helping students succeed. From teachers working together, *a new curriculum emerges* rather than a "hidden" and haphazard curriculum implemented with little coordination in isolated classrooms. The curriculum becomes the result of a collaborative, planned effort targeted to improving student outcomes.

Principals who are consistently responsive, model collaboration, prepare curriculum with teachers, and target student achievement, will over time develop a positive school context and develop a very successful technology program.

Creating Responsive Leadership

Responsive leadership, as opposed to coercive management, permits technology change to be implemented. The principal or school team that "leads" not only provides guidance but works alongside staff and has a vested interest in the results. In contrast, the principal or school team that uses coercive management will tend to dictate orders or make demands of staff and impose punishments when goals are not met. The coercive manager does not have an interest in the process—only in the product. Responsive leadership is probably the only way to obtain a quality program.

Even before reading the research of Edward Deming, developing collaboration and "quality work" was a priority for me as a new principal. Deming (1982), in his research on producing quality, has shown the business world a better way. Through his "Ten Points," Deming taught the Japanese to achieve high quality at low cost when they had a terrible reputation for cheap products. He taught the Japanese the methods for producing high-quality products. Deming originally offered his methods to U.S. automobile CEOs, who rejected them. His methods were accepted in Japan, however, with the result that Japan, for a period of time, dominated the U.S. car market. Even today, the United States is still playing catch-up with Japan's level of car production.

Glasser (1990) has applied the principles proposed by Deming to education in his humanistic view of leadership called Lead Management. The essence of lead management is to motivate teachers toward "quality work" through persuasion and problem solving. The Leader Manager seeks to help the organization run efficiently so that workers will see that it is to their benefit to do quality work. The bulk of the responsibility to improve the system is on the administrator; as teachers are motivated to do quality work, all students will produce quality work.

The essential elements of lead management follow:

- The leader manager engages teachers in a discussion of quality work to be done in the school and the time needed to do the work. The leader provides teachers a chance to add their input.

- The leader manager (or designee) shows or models the job so that the teacher who is to perform the job can see exactly what the leader manager expects. In addition, teachers are continually asked for their input as to how the job can be done better.

- The leader manager asks teachers to inspect or evaluate their own work for quality, with the understanding that the leader will listen and accept that teachers know a great deal about how to produce high-quality work.

- The leader manager is a facilitator in that he or she shows the teachers that everything possible has been done to provide them with the best tools and workplace as well as a noncoercive, nonadversarial atmosphere in which to do their job. (see Glasser, 1990, pp. 31-32)

Lead management fosters the development of collegial habits (Little, 1982) that will bring administrators and teachers together. Innovative practices develop from collegial norms as the leader manager and teachers together solve problems (Reksten, 1995). Instead of the *I* of boss management, the term *we* is used in lead management. Instead of fixing blame on teachers, creating a fear of reprisals within the school, leader managers concentrate on fixing mistakes, creating the confidence to try new technologies.

With lead management in place, the school context will begin to change and staff members will come together into an effective team. The following elements will evidence the effects of lead management:

- Habits of collaboration will be evident. Teachers will regularly participate with each other to plan, share ideas, and discuss how to improve instruction.

- Innovative ideas will be generated by teachers working collaboratively to solve problems. Teachers will be willing to try new ideas when there is a schoolwide support system.

- There will be evidence of shared vision. The staff will feel they are part of the overall mission of the school and value their individual contributions.

- There will be a commitment to performance rather than participation. Teachers will experience intrinsic satisfaction from their work.

- Effort toward school goals will be evaluated by staff. Suggestions for improvement from any staff member will be valued. A course of action will be taken to improve the school based on a staff consensus.

When I was a young principal 13 years ago, the research on effective schools influenced me to think seriously about building a collaborative team so our school could improve student achievement (Lanier & Little, 1986). The research pointed to critical variables that needed to be present in the school context to empower teachers to help students learn: (a) a *supportive collegial group* that contributes ideas and provides assistance where needed so that the goals of student learning are achieved; (b) the exchange of ideas from collegial interaction that gives rise to *innovation* leading to increased effectiveness and greater personal rewards; (c) *a school community* characterized by a distinct vision, clearly articulated goals, and a shared value system embraced by teachers; (d) the *leadership of principals* whose vision is to improve student achievement and convey the certainty to teachers that this achievement can be attained; and (e) the *responsiveness of principals* in buffering teachers, monitoring progress, and supplying additional technical assistance so that teachers can see that they are affecting student achievement (Reksten, 1995).

In an effective school context, this school team works with an organized curriculum to produce a product—student work that demonstrates integrated skills. Such student work will occur when curriculum is organized by concepts and integrated technology skills are used by students to demonstrate understanding. This kind of result with students came to Walt Disney School only after years of building a positive school context, encouraging teachers to take risks, helping teachers visualize the benefits for students, and celebrating our successes along the way. An example of using technology to develop integrated skills is the fourth-grade multimedia project at Walt Disney School—an interactive book. This project requires students to do several integrated tasks:

- Write a story
- Edit and rewrite the story several times
- Develop a story board by dividing the story into parts
- Illustrate each part with pictures
- Scan each picture into the computer using a scanner
- Import each picture onto HyperStudio cards
- Color each picture on each card using art tools
- Type the text for each picture card
- Animate parts of the picture through buttons
- Read and record the story into the computer
- Add music and sound

Any fourth-grade student completing this project is demonstrating his or her learning by practicing the language arts process skills beyond the use of paper and pencil. These process skills will be required in the workplace of tomorrow.

Where We Started at Walt Disney School

Walt Disney School, a 1997 California Distinguished School, wasn't very distinguished when I arrived in 1986. Prior leadership had left the school in a shambles. Teachers were very far from any thought of collaboration, and emphasis on student achievement was not a collective viewpoint. The school context was negative, to say the least. However, 11 years later we were distinguished in all the areas that had been deficit—a positive school context, collaboration, curriculum, and technology. This process did not happen overnight. Over the first 5 years, a positive school context emerged and that led to the development of a unified curriculum and the model technology program that we are known for today.

When I arrived at Walt Disney School as the new principal, the school context was adversarial, with many factions, and teachers were isolated, the epitome of Lortie's (1975) description. Teachers were individualistic in their viewpoints and there was very little collaborative effort. It was even difficult to work together on small committee assignments. Teachers found it hard to trust or even to talk to one another. It soon became my goal to develop a collaborative context where teachers trusted one another and shared a common vision for students.

I realized that the place to begin was with teachers who wanted to work collaboratively. This group became the Leadership Team. Time was spent listening to and encouraging these teachers as well as the others. As a new principal, I listened to their suggestions and began to respond to their needs. As teachers expressed ideas, I gave the teachers power to implement their ideas and share in leadership roles. As I trusted them, they began to trust one another and a seed of collaboration began to grow.

Ten years ago, the Walt Disney School Leadership Team began to visualize using technology to help students improve in their writing. When I first arrived at Disney, there wasn't even a copy machine to use. I remember using the ditto machine to produce my first parent letters and staff bulletins, which were typed on my college typewriter. We were very far away from the model technology school we are today.

We were also a very small (320 students) and a very poor school. In California, small equates to very little money since revenue is created by the number of students in the school (Proposition 13). We were also very diverse, with 8 languages and 30% of our population limited in English, and were steadily growing with more limited-English students. We were beginning to face what we saw as a real crisis in the growing numbers of limited-English students and the complexities of providing effective instruction for this population.

Our dream began in 1987 when I was working in a doctoral program at UCLA. The volume of written papers required necessitated the purchase of a computer and printer. This new computer took up residence in my office where I began to use it to write papers for my coursework and produce written communications for Disney School. Almost immediately, teachers began to comment on the quality of the documents and letters. We began to ask ourselves, "What would happen if students could use computers for their written work?" It was at that point that we started to visualize and develop a plan using only a few Apple IIes and my office computer. We had no idea where we would obtain the funds to buy computers.

Preparing for Our Technology Program

We thought it would be a good idea to do some research. At first, we invited an Apple Computer representative to show us what was current in technology and what we might want to purchase. Because we wanted our students to improve in writing, the Apple representative showed us a "Writing and Publishing Hardware and Software Bundle" that included a scanner, laser printer, file server, and eight Macintosh SE 20 computers. We needed a basic word processing program for students. I was already using Microsoft Works, which had four different programs for school office documents. The leadership team and I decided this program would be the best investment for the money.

In addition, the Apple representative talked with us about using a file server to keep track of student files instead of using disks. It just made sense from the beginning that we wanted to use a file server instead of managing more than 300 disks for students. However, we had no idea how to set up or manage a file server. We also learned that the Macintosh could easily link the file server to other Macintosh computers. Therefore, we would not need to spend money on special networking, which we didn't understand at that time anyway.

We didn't depend on only Apple to give us direction. We also went to Lockheed, a neighbor of ours in Burbank, for advice. After touring their graphic arts department, we discovered that they were converting all their computers from IBM to Macintosh because of the ease of use and the graphics capacities of the Macintosh. We thought that they would recommend IBM, but they strongly advised us to purchase Macintoshes and argued that they would be easier for students to use, especially limited-English students.

We also visited Emery Park School, a model elementary technology school in Alhambra that had received a very large grant from the state of California. On that visit, I took the most skeptical staff members as well as more favorable staff. We visited several classrooms and saw how computers were placed within the school (lab and classroom), how the computers were being used, and listened to the principal's and teachers' philosophy. We saw students using remedial practice programs. We determined right away that we would not use drill and practice programs with students because these programs allow very little flexibility with curriculum and are "closed-ended." We wanted the computer to be used as a tool for curriculum projects rather than a separate drill and practice program. Most important, though, we decided from that visit what technology we would buy and wouldn't buy. For example, we saw that the Apple IIGS was very slow in accessing programs and student work and decided against buying that computer in favor of a faster Macintosh.

One of the key decisions we made as a result of the visit was a configuration for a computer lab. Our goal was to provide the greatest amount of access to students although we knew that we would not be able to buy a large number of computers. Deciding on a combination of 13 computers and a work area for students was a step toward a complete lab with 30 computers.

Developing Our Technology Plan

After returning to Disney from our visit, we began to plan where we might locate this lab. Since we wanted the lab to be in the center of the school for the greatest security, we chose a central classroom. I remember taking the Leadership Team into this room, designated as "The Disney Writing and Publishing Lab," and visualizing with them where equipment might be located in the configuration we had talked about.

To use this room, we knew that we would have to give up our curriculum resource room and reorganize our teaching resource materials. Because teachers had already embraced the vision of technology for students, there was a willingness to reorganize the resource room. I suspect their reaction may not have been so positive if they had not been working collaboratively together. These decisions were made by staff when we did not know where the money for technology was coming from.

In 1989, our Budget Director informed us of a one-time amount of School Improvement Supplemental Grant money (based on enrollment) available to each School Improvement school. It required the development of a plan. Since we already had a plan for our technology program, we quickly completed our plan during April 1989 so that we could buy the equipment during the summer for staff training. We also planned for additional electrical outlets, relocation of desks, and security doors to be completed during the summer.

The teaching staff volunteered their time for the 3-day training on Microsoft Works 1.0 during the summer. The staff felt that as we were spending the $25,000 of supplemental grant money on computer technology, it was important to learn how to use the equipment. In return for attending the training, staff members took the computers home to practice the skills they had learned. One brave classroom teacher began working with her students in our new computer lab with our new computers during October 1989. From her experiences, as well as those of other Disney teachers who followed into our new lab, we started our journey toward improving the writing of students.

Start With Students in Mind

The first place to begin building a strong technology program at your school is with your students. What do you believe about the value of technology for your students? How will technology assist the learning of your students? What do your staff members believe about the value of technology for students? If your program is not founded on the impact technology will have on the learning of your students, then your program will not be successful.

We started with a focus on improving the writing skills of our limited-English students. As a result, our first Mission Statement in 1989 read:

Mission Statement 1989

Students will use computer technology to apply elements of the writing process to formulate and communicate ideas through the production of illustrated published products in a lab setting.

Our most recent Mission Statement in 1998 is very similar; however, it is greatly expanded in focus.

Mission Statement 1998

The Disney staff strongly believes that all students must have access to a technology-enhanced curriculum so that they can manage and find information, communicate and produce meaningful products for living in a global society.

In 1989 we were focused on the development of language arts skills. By 1998 we were more targeted toward using technology skills and the language arts process skills across all curricular areas. We firmly believe that these process skills, along with integrated technology skills, will be skills that are easily transferable to any level of school or future work for our students.

What are the needs of your students? How can technology assist in meeting these needs? This is the very best place to begin before doing anything else. Schools often begin by buying equipment before they have decided how it will help their students. A focus on student needs will also help you forge your staff into a unified team since the baseline motivation for all educators is helping students learn.

Develop Your Student Expectancies

The next level of planning with students in mind is the development of student expectancies or realistic goals that are achievable. A mission statement has a broad focus, whereas an expectancy is a tangible goal that helps to narrow the focus and provide meaning to the mission statement. To develop expectancies, schools must ask a very basic question: "How do we want students specifically to use technology?" In developing the expectancies for Walt Disney School, we defined what we meant by our mission statement.

In 1989, our student expectancies were:

- Students will experience a meaningful context of today's business world.

- Students will learn the basic process of research and writing as well as working in cooperative groups to integrate these skills to publish their works.

In 1998, our student expectancies were:

- All students will become competent in using technology as a tool to enhance curriculum projects that support the integration of process skills in oral and written communication, calculating, problem solving, researching, organizing, and the presentation of information.

- All students will learn to access and utilize Internet resources for technology-enhanced curriculum projects cooperatively, ethically, and collaboratively.

- All students will have opportunities to produce and share their technology-enhanced curriculum projects cooperatively, ethically, and collaboratively.

In 1989, our focus was on improving the writing process and on publishing student work. Our emphasis also included helping students to work in cooperative teams, as in the business world, whereas our expanded emphasis is now on using language arts process skills and technology as tools across all areas of curriculum. Students are learning how to research, organize, and present information as well as to communicate in a variety of formats instead of strictly in a written format. Students are also working in cooperative teams, paralleling the business world.

Align Student Benchmarks

When your school has determined a mission statement and student expectancies, student benchmarks or specific targets for your program must be identified. We have formulated those targets on two levels: (a) benchmarks for all students; and (b) benchmarks by grade levels. In order to develop benchmarks, begin by finishing the statement, "All students of _____ School will . . ." The following are our 1998 benchmarks for all students:

All students of Walt Disney School will:

- Apply a variety of software applications to the creation of grade-level curriculum projects in Language Arts, Math, Science, History/Social Science, and Fine Arts.

- Develop and apply the Language Arts skills of listening, reading, writing, and speaking in grade-level technology projects. These projects will also demonstrate the use and development of the writing process (research, prewriting, drafting, editing, revising, and publishing).

- Use technology as a tool to integrate curricular areas in their technology projects.

- Access and analyze reference information within curriculum in a variety of media formats using CD-ROM, animation, video, and television media, telecommunications with educators, research agencies, and access current information on the World Wide Web.

- Regularly access Internet resources on the World Wide Web, CD-ROM, video, and television media for curriculum projects, communicate with educational research agencies to obtain and share current data (e.g., NASA Spacelink, Ask a Geologist, Ask ERIC, Getty Arts Ed Net, etc.), and download research data (text, pictures, graphics, QuickTime movies, video) for curriculum projects through the World Wide Web.

- Be provided opportunities to develop the thinking skills of application, synthesis, analysis, evaluation, and meta-cognition through the completion of technology-enhanced curriculum projects.

- Apply, analyze, synthesize, and evaluate curricular information in a variety of multimedia formats using text, graphics, and video (e.g., development of interactive books, creation and maintenance of the Disney Home Page on the Internet).

- Collaborate in heterogeneous groupings to share information and access diverse student talents in the production of technology-enhanced curriculum projects.

- Learn to collaborate and solve problems with other students of diverse cultural backgrounds cooperatively in the creation of technology-enhanced curriculum projects.

Our student benchmarks reflect the targets we want to have achieved with fifth-grade students when they leave Walt Disney Elementary School for middle school. However, there is a more specific breakdown of benchmarks needed by grade level to target more specifically the skills to be developed. We have identified grade-level benchmarks at two levels: (a) Primary—Grades K-2, and Intermediate—Grades 3-5; and (b) specific grade levels, kindergarten through Grade 5. A discussion of specific grade-level technology-enhanced skills with curriculum can be found in Chapter 5 (see "Articulating Technology Skills: Grades K-5"). Following is how we have taken our benchmarks and further targeted them specifically to primary and intermediate grade levels.

Kindergarten-Grade 2

Students will be introduced to a broad range of technology experiences. The introduction should include instruction in basic computer use, such as start-up, opening/closing files and applications, disk management, and appropriate care. Students will learn how to explore or browse through various grade-level-appropriate programs. Also, students will create documents that include pictures and words relating to curricular activities and objectives. Adding voice narration in computer-generated slide shows will enhance video presentations of student artwork.

Grade 3-Grade 5

Students will create presentations, including desktop publishing and hypermedia presentations, to enhance their curricular studies in all areas. Increased proficiency of keyboarding will be expected. Presentations will include carefully selected materials, including scanned, digital camera, or video camera images, along with CD-ROM, QuickTime movies, and Internet resources. Students will learn to communicate by using a converter and video capture tools to create original video presentations that reflect an understanding of curricular objectives. Students will expand their learning community by sharing the curricular projects they produced using HTML and posted on the Disney Home Page and through electronic mail, as well as demonstrate their research and organization of information using the World Wide Web.

The process of narrowing a school's technology mission statement from expectancies to benchmarks at a specific grade level requires time, experience, and much discussion by a school staff. Since our simple mission statement in 1989, we have had 10 years of learning how to use technology with our students. We have learned most often by the mistakes we have made as well as by analyzing student technology projects. It is not necessary to have everything defined and laid out in detail on paper before beginning. You must begin and then learn about using technology along the way. The technology vision your staff has for your students is really written in their minds before it is written on paper.

Identify a School Leadership Team

Through the influence of Deming, Glasser, and others, it became obvious that I must model the characteristics of lead management. This kind of leading would empower teachers to share leadership roles and encourage them to take risks because I was willing to take risks in using technology. One of the strengths of Walt Disney School's technology program that developed from a principal-teacher collaboration was a Technology Leadership Team. This team first included teachers who were using technology or were interested in wanting to learn about technology. On visits to other schools and businesses, we included any staff member who was interested and even those who were somewhat negative about the idea. As with any functioning committee, we made sure that there was staff representation from all groups. At Disney, we included primary teachers, intermediate teachers, office staff, instructional assistants, and students. This group participated in many discussions as we were deciding what would be best for our students. We also visualized what could be done with technology and how it might look in the school without putting a dollar amount to our ideas. We took action when there were funds to implement our basic plan and remained flexible, adjusting our plans along the way.

Be Ready to Take Action

One of the most difficult tasks a leadership team will have is to implement its plans. There is a certain risk in beginning something new. Some school teams have the notion that the circumstances must be perfect before taking action. In any new innovation, "perfect" doesn't exist. It is necessary to jump into the fire, make some mistakes, and find out what kind of adjustments must be made. This process continues over and over until steady uphill progress is made. Staff must be ready for this kind of commitment. It is like running a marathon. Many teachers find this philosophy very threatening and would prefer to be safe. This is the reason for establishing a strong collaborative support base with an encouraging leader manager who is willing to model the risks associated with technology and be a "cheerleader" for those who follow in risk taking. With this type of nonthreatening school context, one in which teachers can feel free to experiment with technology and yet be guaranteed that they will be supported, your technology program will go forward with the support of teachers and the school community to benefit all students in your school.

CHAPTER 3

Focusing the Curriculum With Concept-Based Instruction

···

With or without technology at your school, very little can be accomplished without a concerted effort by school faculty and leadership to lay out the curriculum in a planned and orderly manner to achieve student expectancies. Critical here is truly in-depth planning by your teachers. Too often, too little time is allocated by school leadership for serious preparation of curriculum. There is instead more emphasis on instructional implementation and assessment. However, the curriculum must be the base from which instruction flows and assessment can best function, especially with the onset of new State standards.

With the rate of information now doubling every 6 months, it is becoming increasingly difficult to cover the volume of information exploding into our world. Teachers must distinguish the "essential" from the "nice-to-know" in curriculum. Already most subject matter curricula in school districts continue to swell with more and more to teach and less and less time to teach it. The tendency of most teachers is to try to "teach all of the curriculum" rather than to separate the essential from the nice-to-know. At Disney, we've learned how vital it is to build on a concept framework rather than a fact framework.

The concept framework, which we call Concept-Based Instruction, requires that teachers narrow the curriculum by identifying essential concepts within subject matter domains that will promote student understanding, because teaching by concepts always promotes understanding and relationships for students. Concept-based instruction, then, is a means of providing teachers both a product and a process. The product is the narrowed mandated curriculum, one that is more workable and meaningful for both teachers and students. When this curriculum is developed through a specific planning process and implemented by teachers, students participate in daily activities that construct meaning from the targeted concepts. For example, through the planning process for our schoolwide concept "Culture," one of our concept generalizations is, "People have traditions and ceremonies they pass on to each generation."

Students explore the meanings of "traditions" and "ceremonies" from the context of the generalization through activities and projects rather than simply learning the definitions of the terms.

What Is Concept-Based Instruction?

Once concepts have been identified within curricula, teachers must implement instruction in a way that students can access the understandings of those concepts. Concept-based instruction is a comprehensive approach to classroom instruction that uses integrated learning activities to link concepts, processes, and skills around a core concept. The obvious focus in this kind of instruction is the student, who is then required to construct meaning of the curricular concepts by using processes (e.g., reading, writing) and skills (e.g., comprehension, application). A curriculum that is focused on integrated instruction becomes the ideal venue for the integrated skills of technology.

A mistake that is often made by schools is to approach technology as an entity separate from the "regular curriculum" of art, literature, science, history, social science, and so on. Often technology is perceived to be "a curriculum," therefore it is never really used as an important tool to drive curricular planning and implementation. As a result of this misunderstanding of technology, the tendency in most schools is either to buy technology equipment without considering how it is to be used with students or to buy the equipment to facilitate a specific software program. Either way, the curriculum and definitive student expectancies are rarely considered. Technology as described becomes additive and unrelated to the curriculum rather than integrated with the curriculum.

Concept-Based Instruction Develops Process Skills

Concept-based instruction links prior instruction to new instruction. Student understanding is built through a "layering effect" as more and more associations are constructed in the brain (Wolfe, 1998). When curriculum is not focused, there is a tendency to teach isolated facts without building concept relationships. As a result, the layering of understandings and connections in the brain is not as effectively established for long-term memory. In addition, teaching facts in isolation, without creating understanding through concepts, does not challenge the thinking of learners at the analysis, synthesis, and evaluative levels.

The thinking skills we want students to develop that are transferable to any future employment are referred to as "process skills." These skills include the language arts skills of listening, speaking, reading, and writing; the mathematical skills of computing and solving problems; and the various levels of thinking skills that cut across curriculum content areas (science, history/social science, etc.) and include comprehending, applying, analyzing, synthesizing, and evaluating.

Integrating technology into the curriculum furthers the development of these process skills in students since technology skills are themselves integrated. For example, the basic functions of turning on the computer, accessing files, and opening and manipulating a program application to do work involve many integrated tasks. When technology is used as a tool in the same way paper and pencil are used, students continuously practice integrated skills when doing work in a curricular area. In addition, technology assists students to do projects within the curriculum that have never been possible before because of the limitations of paper and pencil.

Daggett, in his July 1998 speech to California administrators and teachers, stressed the importance of developing process skills for the application of knowledge for the new jobs in the 21st century. Daggett identified three types of knowledge—declarative, procedural, and process—to illustrate the importance of separating essential from nice-to-know information. Declarative knowledge is the essential facts of curriculum. Procedural knowledge, on the other hand, is the reading, writing, and computational skills a student uses to access information. Process knowledge is the ability to associate, adapt, and apply knowledge. According to Daggett, "Our kids do not know how to process because we major in declarative instruction" (Daggett, 1998). Unfortunately, the process level is rarely addressed in instructional decision making as we continue to drown students in a sea of facts to cover the mandated curriculum instead of helping students build connections through concepts. The real world demands that students have the ability to associate, adapt, and apply knowledge in the solving of real-world problems.

Why Concept-Based Instruction and Curriculum?

Why go to all the trouble to organize a concept-based curriculum rather than be guided by a framework of facts? First, learning occurs best when concepts and activities are integrated, as they are in life. Every task in life is an integrated task rather than a departmentalized task. Think about the skills you use to balance your checkbook, drive your car, write a letter, and more. All of these tasks involve a complicated integration of brain and muscle functions that are not separate in execution.

Second, concept-based curriculum links core subjects around concepts or central ideas. Traditionally, curricular disciplines have been departmentalized and scheduled from hour to hour. This outdated organization of curriculum lends itself to the teaching of facts without establishing a basis for how these facts relate to each other and to other disciplines.

Now, with 12 languages at Walt Disney School, we have seen our students link schoolwide "concepts" to curricular areas. For example, the broad concept of Culture, with supporting concepts articulated at all grade levels, assists in maintaining a curricular flow for specific kinds of grouping, such as those students in special education and the English language learners. Students being pulled for special services are supported by the concept organization embraced by the school. The curriculum in the regular education classroom is linked with the curriculum in the special education classroom because we've found that concept organization of the curriculum supports the inclusion of all students in the curriculum.

Third, concept organization and its attendant concept-based instruction/teaching emphasize the use of skills and processes for constructing meaning and solving problems. The goal becomes to illuminate more clearly the concept under study through the problems or issues contained within concepts resident in content area curricula. For example, grade-level concepts formed into generalizations and essential understandings provide targets for developing student understanding. This kind of teaching prepares students to apply and use what they are learning not only within a discipline, but between disciplines and to predictable real-world problems.

Fourth, concept organization/teaching allows for more effective use of instructional time. When teachers are able to identify concepts within disciplines/domains and coordinate concepts across curricular areas, instructional time becomes focused and integrated. At the same time, instructional time no longer emphasizes knowing the facts, but uses facts to develop an understanding of concepts.

Fifth, concept organization/teaching contributes to an interdisciplinary rather than a multidisciplinary curriculum. *Interdisciplinary* refers to organizing curricular disciplines so that they share a common concept focus. This common focus contributes to building a deeper understanding of problems and issues in the minds of students, thus making connections and building understandings. At Walt Disney School, we use science or history/social science content as a concept organizer for other curricular areas such as literature, art, health, music, and so on. For example, with the concept "Change," our fourth grade explores how the Gold Rush brought significant change to California settlements. The organization includes a concept generalization for this fourth-grade unit, "The Gold Rush in California brought about changes that continue to shape California's future today," that weaves facts into concept understandings that have meaning for students.

In comparison, multidisciplinary curricula lack concept focus because they relate facts and activities across subject areas to common topics such as "bears," "the ocean," or "plants." When teachers teach by topic, there is a tendency to focus on facts, which do not relate to essential understandings. The curriculum becomes fragmented and lacks meaning, and it is difficult for students to adapt and apply the knowledge. Unfortunately, a majority of schools use declarative (factual) knowledge as an instructional base rather than teach students how to associate and apply knowledge through an interdisciplinary, concept-based curriculum to real-life problems in our world (Daggett, 1998).

Another problem with multidisciplinary curriculum is the overriding tendency to cover the entire curriculum. MidContinent Regional Education Laboratory (McREL), a U.S. Department of Education research organization in Colorado, has identified 255 standards across all curriculum areas. A Gallup study reported by Daggett in a conference to California administrators in July 1998 stated that teachers ran out of time at the end of the school year covering only 132 standards (Daggett, 1998), leaving 123 standards not covered. In addition, the Third International Mathematics and Science Study (TIMSS) reported that American teachers taught 78 topics per year as compared with Japanese teachers, who taught 17 topics, or German teachers with 23 topics. Surely it is not just a coincidence that both Japan and Germany had significantly higher scores in math and science than the United States. There must indeed be some inhibiting effect on student learning that originates from an ever-growing curriculum mandated by most states. Hence, a school that spends time narrowing and focusing curriculum through concepts can best prepare students for tomorrow's workforce.

Finally, curriculum organized by concepts allows students to work at appropriate developmental levels. The science concepts of "change," "energy," or "interdependence" can be accessed through understandings of concepts rather than through isolated facts with few relationships. Teaching facts alone will not provide meaning for students. Dimensions of complexity are added to core concepts such as Culture through successive grades as each grade level approaches this concept through curriculum. For example, our fifth grade looks at the colonization of America as a part of our schoolwide emphasis on Culture. The concept of colonization is not mastered in fifth grade; it will continue to be developed at other grade levels with different curricula. The understanding of concepts is additive and will continue to develop across a lifetime of learning.

What Is the Concept-Based Curriculum?

The concept-based curriculum has several critical components. The first layer consists of identifying core concepts, grade-level concepts from mandated curriculum, essential understandings, guided questions, and student expectancies. Based on the first layer, the second layer of concept-based curriculum involves webbing across curricular areas, articulating identified concepts across grade levels, and assessment of concept acquisition (see Figure 3.1).

Concepts are the primary organizers of a concept-based curriculum. The place to begin is with a *core concept* or "Big Idea." Possible core concepts can include: Change, Culture, Democracy, Energy, Government, Family, Stability, and many others. Each of these Big Ideas encompasses

Figure 3.1. The Concept-Based Curriculum

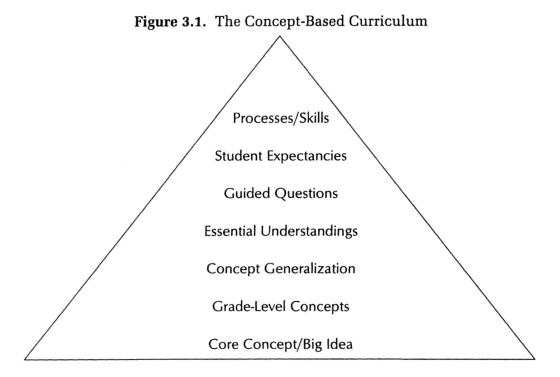

several concepts from various curricula. Identifying concepts from grade-level content curricula (usually science or history/social science) helps to generalize a Big Idea to *Grade-Level Concepts*. After grade-level concepts are identified, concept generalizations can be formulated. A *Concept Generalization* is a statement that puts two or more concepts in relationship to the area of study.

From concept generalizations, *essential understandings* can be determined. Essential understandings are statements of grade-level concepts that are critical and that students must understand at a given grade level. Essential understandings provide the basis for *Guided Questions*, which help students explore the concept generalizations. When answering these questions, students are required to apply processes and skills that in turn contribute to the development of the essential understandings. These processes and skills include the language arts and math skills, thinking skills, and technology skills. In essence, processes and skills serve to help students develop understanding from guided questions. guided questions lead to the expectations we have for student achievement. This achievement is stated in terms of *Student Expectancies* or a demonstrated result we expect to see from students.

Once the concept-based curriculum components have been planned, *Webbing* can be done to plan across curricular areas. Typically, webbing is used by many teachers when planning topical studies, such as "bears" or "plants," rather than with a conceptual study such as "culture." Teachers are very familiar with using a topic and planning activities in other curricular areas around that topic. The problem with this kind of webbing is that it is very difficult to relate these topics to a higher-order concept. Hence student study ends up focusing on facts. However, when webbing is combined with a concept-based curriculum that has identified essential understandings, guided questions, processes and skills, and student expectancies, students gain a deep understanding of content and concepts across the curriculum.

Once each grade level has planned its concept-based curriculum, articulation of these concepts across the grades clarifies for teachers the development of the core concept throughout the school. *Articulation* refers to making teachers aware of what other teachers are teaching at various grade levels. This process helps to build understanding and unity within the school around the core concept and aligns the grade-level expectancies.

Finally, *assessment* of concept-based curriculum is ultimately based on how well students answer the guided questions at each grade level. Student expectancies are based on guided questions defined by grade level. How well students demonstrate understanding of grade-level concepts can be assessed through grade-level rubrics.

Translating Concepts to Essential Understandings

With the essential understandings in mind, teachers at Walt Disney School gather in grade-level groupings with the curriculum from all subject areas and select grade-level concepts under the umbrella of our schoolwide concepts (e.g., Change). Concepts are selected that "thread" through two or more curricular areas. Then, the grade-level concepts are worded as generalizations (Figure 3.2). For example, with the grade-level concept Change, our fourth-grade teachers developed this generalization:

> The Gold Rush in California brought about **changes** that continue to shape California's future today.

The grade-level concept Change is then related to what it is essential for the student to learn—conflicts, cooperation, and the shaping of events concerning the early settlement of California. According to Erickson (1995), such relationships are titled "Essential Understandings" and form the critical content of the curriculum. From our generalization on Change, the following essential understandings were developed:

- Change leads to conflicts and cooperation that contribute to growth in various areas
- Change leads to conflict
- Change leads to cooperation
- Change is an ongoing process that shapes a civilization's future
- The resulting growth becomes the next change

Figure 3.2. Concept-Based Curriculum Planning, Grade 4

Core Concept: Change   **Unit Generalization:** The Gold Rush in California brought   **Grade:** 4
about changes that continue to shape California's future today.

Essential Understandings	Guided Questions	Student Expectancies	Student Processes/Skills
1. Change leads to conflicts and cooperation that contribute to growth in various areas.	What do you know about the Gold Rush?	1. Students will compare the life of the settlers before the Gold Rush and after.	Read Compare Contrast
2. Change leads to conflict.	What changes occurred as a result of the Gold Rush?	2. Students will identify three main conflicts that occurred as a result of the Gold Rush, and compare those to life in California today.	Analyze Compare Communicate Write
3. Conflict leads to cooperation.	How does change lead to growth?		
4. Change, an ongoing process, shapes a civilization's future.	How did the population of California change?	3. Students will create a HyperStudio stack using Internet resources on one important change that resulted from the Gold Rush and how that change affects California today.	Design Research Communicate Write
5. The resulting growth becomes the next change.	What conflicts arose from these changes? How were these conflicts resolved?		

SOURCE: Used with permission of Roberta Smith.

The planning process continues and science or history/social science are used as primary organizers for developing schoolwide concepts. Very often, math can be easily integrated with science concepts, or history/ social science can integrate well with literature, art, and music. However, not all areas of the curriculum need to be integrated or must be integrated. It is simply an easier way to narrow and target the curriculum instead of basing the curriculum on a sea of disjointed facts.

Formulating Guided Questions

Once essential understandings have been formulated, guided questions are developed. These questions are used to develop essential understandings beyond the lower-level thinking skills of fact-finding to higher-level understandings (Erickson, 1995, 1998). In our fourth-grade Gold Rush example, guided questions were developed, including, "What changes occurred as a result of the Gold Rush?" and "How does change lead to growth?" We found the use of guided questions helps to elevate the thinking of students. Guided questions can be structured at the comprehension level of thinking and increase in complexity to encourage the application, synthesis, and evaluation levels of thinking. Refer to Figure 3.2 for examples of fourth-grade guided questions.

Guided questions, by design, stimulate the interest and thinking of learners. In the 1960s, instructional objective statements would normally have been the focus for learners (Mager, 1975). However, instructional objectives have a tendency to focus on facts and the covering of information rather than on building understanding and meaning through the relationship of concepts. Questions are by nature more stimulating to learners and provoke more thinking, as opposed to a statement of learning intent.

Identifying Student Expectancies

Once guided questions are developed, student expectancies are formulated. These should be based on the state content standards and the benchmarks developed by your state or school district. "Benchmarks are statements of developmental levels of information and skill that define the general categories of knowledge articulated by the standards" (Marzano & Kendall, 1996, p. 47). In other words, benchmarks are statements of specific information and skills that students are to know and to be able to do. Benchmarks, as used here, are synonymous with student expectancies.

Benchmarks can be "declarative," as in expecting students to understand the terms and concepts of the California Gold Rush. Benchmarks can also be "procedural," as in expecting students to perform skills, strategies, and processes in designing a HyperStudio presentation using Internet research to present an important change that resulted from the California Gold Rush and its impact on California today.

The last part of the planning process is to identify student expectancies based on state-adopted standards and benchmarks. Student expectancies are statements of what you want students to be able to know (declarative) or to be able to do or perform (procedural or process), applied across curriculum. Students' meeting of expectancies reflects a level of understanding and application of the essential understandings as assessed through multiple measures (tests, portfolios of work in progress, writing samples, oral presentations, technology projects, etc.).

Student expectancies are identified by each teacher. There must be a clear understanding of what students are expected to know and to do. Expectancies focus on a student's ability to solve problems, think, and communicate when given complex tasks. Because expectancies focus on individual performance rather than group comparisons, the developmental needs of students can be met.

Let me point out that this focus on student expectancies dramatically changes the role of the teacher in the classroom. The teacher becomes a *facilitator*, guiding students through the learning process, creating the appropriate learning environment, and making instructional decisions based on student needs and the development of process skills. The emphasis is not solely on the dispensing of knowledge, but also on helping students construct meaning from what they are learning and apply this learning to real-life situations. As students construct meaning, they develop their language arts and math process skills as well as other thinking skills. Thus students integrate both knowledge and skills. It is in the context of a targeted curriculum focused on student expectancies that technology becomes an ideal fit.

Technology, by nature, is a tool that is integrated. From turning on the computer, to opening a software program, to performing in that program, all skills are integrated. It demands that the user make decisions, perform functions, and produce a product. All software programs are performance driven. A concept-based curriculum that requires students to participate in performance activities to produce a product as a student measure aligns well with the integrated nature of technology.

The Process of Concept-Based Planning

Providing time for staff to participate in Concept-Based Planning is a must for your teachers. This process is twofold and requires the orchestration of planning time for your teachers in grade-level teams. During the first part of the process, teachers must identify grade-level concepts from curriculum and formulate generalizations from concepts. These generalizations constitute the essential understandings of the study. Guided questions are constructed to draw learners into the study. Student expectancies are then planned with the process skills that students will use to create meaning from concepts.

The second part of the planning process involves webbing (see Figure 3.3) to weave in other areas of the curriculum. Once the essential understandings of the study have been clearly identified, teachers can identify the common conceptual threads in other curricula. These conceptual threads then guide the selection of literature, writing, fine arts activities, technology projects, and the use of other resources. When each grade level has finished the planning process, articulation of grade-level concepts across all grades will build schoolwide unity for the study. Articulation helps teachers see the schoolwide scope of the study and elevates the importance of each grade level as a vital part. Finally, assessment of student expectancies for grade levels and multilevels examines the depth of concept understanding and assists in refining future curriculum.

Concept-Based Planning Steps

At Disney, we use 11 steps to complete our planning process for each core concept or Big Idea.

Figure 3.3. Concept Webbing

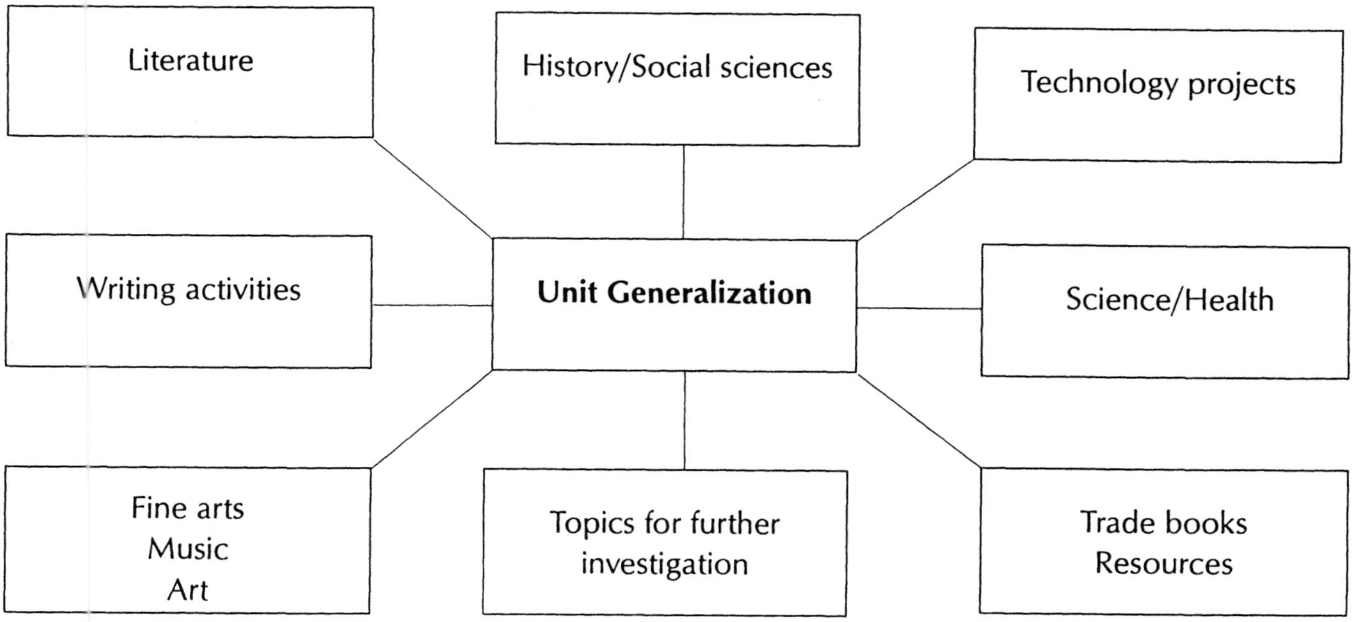

Step 1: Select Schoolwide Core Concepts

Select schoolwide core concepts that are Big Ideas. These big ideas must stretch over the course of grade-level curricula of either history/ social science or science. Our school Leadership Team first selected Culture, with the consensus of staff, as a Big Idea during the beginning of the 1993 school year. Culture fit well with the history/social science curriculum across all grade levels. Disney staff decided that along with the core concept Culture, a schoolwide multicultural emphasis would be implemented from January to March. With 50% of our students limited in English, staff felt strongly about selecting Culture as a schoolwide core concept. Finally, a multicultural evening was also planned to reach out to parents.

The Leadership Team also was convinced that training was necessary for all staff to learn how to do concept-based planning. In September 1993, two afternoon faculty meetings were set aside to train teachers in this process. Teachers were trained in organizing integrated curriculum, recognizing grade-level concepts in their curriculum, and writing concept generalizations, essential understandings, guided questions, and student expectancies as a result of their study of these concepts. Teachers then learned how to integrate art, music, literature, and other curricular areas into their grade-level curricula. Additional training was given in mapping out instruction across a 2- to 4-week time frame and developing writing prompts to test the acquisition and understanding of these grade-level concepts. Grade-level writing prompts (see Figure 3.4) based on students'

Figure 3.4. Grade 3 Culture Writing Prompt

The purpose of this prompt is for students to compare the culture of
one tribe of Native Americans with the culture of another tribe of
Native Americans.

The prompt is to be given using the following steps:

1. Students will refer to the table they made comparing four cultures
   to discuss how each of these cultures were alike and different.
   Ideas will be recorded on paragraph trees (graphic organizer).

2. Students will select one Native American tribe and describe the
   similarities and differences of its culture with today's California
   culture. The first paragraph will describe similarities and the
   second paragraph will describe differences. The teacher will
   model how to use a graphic organizer to generate the two
   paragraphs.

3. Students will then select two different Native American tribes and
   write one paragraph of similarities and one paragraph of
   differences.

---

understanding of the concept Culture and the scoring of these prompts
through using a rubric were put into place to measure concept acquisition
and writing mechanics. This measure became the basis of establishing a
schoolwide portfolio system.

Step 2: Schedule Grade-Level Planning

The planning of concepts requires a great deal of time. Providing time
for planning, either through substitutes or use of pupil free days, is the responsibility of the principal. After initial training of the Disney staff to
plan for the Culture concept, grade-level teams of teachers participated in a
morning planning session. Substitutes were paid to release teachers from
classrooms. In the planning session, teachers completed plans, including
several graphic organizers that took the teachers through the process.

Step 3: Identify Grade-Level
Concepts From Curriculum

It is important for teachers to learn to separate concepts from topics.
Most teachers have a tendency to teach from topics, which reduces in-
struction to facts, rather than to teach concepts that build understandings.
For example, "bears" is a common topic used in kindergarten as it relates

to various stories; however, the concept of "community" can build understandings of family, heritage, friends, and more.

Step 4: Formulate Generalizations From Identified Concepts

In order to write a concept generalization, teachers must word key concepts as statements that will guide instruction. For example, the fifth-grade generalization for Culture is, "The American people then and now are people of many races, religions, and national origins who live under a common government." A generalization is a way for teachers to focus their instruction around key concepts.

Step 5: Identify Essential Understandings

Teachers then formulate essential understandings to establish a relationship among concepts. For example, teachers developed the second-grade unit generalization, "All living things have life cycles and experience changes" (Figure 3.5). The essential understandings developed from the concept Change include:

- All plants have parts that have a function
- Plant growth depends on specific conditions
- Different conditions determine the rate of plant growth
- All organisms change through life cycles
- Organisms exhibit change at each stage of development

Step 6: Write Guided Questions

Guided questions are developed from essential understandings. They are designed to interest the learner and to challenge the learner at various levels of thinking, from the basic comprehension levels to the analysis, synthesis, and evaluation levels. These questions are posted in the classroom and answered through the study of the grade-level concepts. For example, some of the guided questions associated with the second-grade unit on life cycles included:

- What are the basic parts of a plant? (Comprehension)
- What are the conditions necessary for plants to grow? (Comprehension)
- How do different growth conditions affect plants? (Analysis)
- How is the life cycle of plants similar/different to the life cycle of animals? (Analysis, Synthesis)

Figure 3.5. Concept-Based Curriculum Planning, Grade 2

Core Concept: Change.	Unit Generalization: All living things demonstrate change through life cycles.		Grade: 2
Essential Understandings	*Guided Questions*	*Student Expectancies*	*Student Process/Skills*
1. All plants have parts that have a function.	What are the parts of a plant? How do different parts function?	1. Observe, compare, and contrast lima bean seeds through keeping a log.	Observe Compare Write
2. Plant growth depends on specific conditions. Different conditions determine the rate of growth.	What conditions are necessary for plants to grow? How do different conditions affect plants?	2. Create a model of the parts of a plant used to create seeds.	Draw Write Label
3. All organisms change through life cycles.	What is a life cycle? What are the characteristics of each stage in a life cycle? How is the life cycle of plants different from that of animals?	3. Compare and contrast the life cycles of a butterfly and a plant using a Venn diagram. Illustrate and write using the computer.	Compare Contrast Draw Write Word Process
4. Organisms exhibit change at each stage of development.	What are the similarities and differences in the life cycles of organisms? What is symmetry?	4. Keep a log of the developmental changes observed in butterflies, frogs, and fruit flies.	Write Discuss Analyze
	How does symmetry change at each stage in the life cycle of an organism?	5. Create a slide show illustrating developmental changes.	Sequence Write Illustrate

SOURCE: Used with permission of Judith Doerflinger.

Step 7: Develop Student Expectancies

Once guided questions have been formed, student expectancies are developed. Again, such expectancies are available from state/district standards and should be utilized in teachers' planning. Some of the student expectancies developed for our second grade during the schoolwide concept Change are:

- Students will observe, compare, and contrast lima bean seeds with peanut seeds through keeping a log

- Students will demonstrate their understanding of the parts in a flower necessary to produce seeds by creating a model

- Students will compare and contrast the life cycles of a butterfly and a plant using a Venn diagram, and illustrate this understanding using the computer

- Students will keep a log of the developmental changes observed in butterflies, frogs, and fruit flies
- Students will create a slide show using the computer to illustrate developmental changes

Student expectancies developed from grade-level concepts should measure a student's basic knowledge and understanding of concepts through performance activities that utilize language arts skills as well as technology skills. These expectancies are integrated tasks that require students to use process skills in order to demonstrate their understanding.

Step 8: Identify Skills and Processes (Strategies) That Learners Will Use in Comprehending and Creating Meaning

It is helpful for teachers to identify the processes and skills that students will develop. Often in student expectancies teachers don't differentiate between declarative knowledge and understandings we want students to know and the processes students will use to access that information. Teachers must see themselves as developers of both declarative knowledge organized by concepts and the process skills students will need to access information. The following science processes identify skills necessary to develop student understanding and stretch thinking to higher levels. These processes are used throughout the science field.

- Observing—"What do you see?"
- Communicating—"Plot the data on a graph."
- Comparing—"How are these alike/different?"
- Ordering—"What patterns are here?"
- Categorizing—"Identify the similar groups."
- Relating—"What caused this to happen?"
- Inferring—"What can you infer from the data?"

Our second-grade teachers identified the processes and skills that students would develop as a result of studying the concepts related to the changes in life cycles (refer to Figure 3.5).

Step 9: Integrate Other Curricular Areas by Webbing

Once the grade-level concepts, essential understandings, guided questions, and student expectancies are formed, *Webbing* occurs. Webbing is the process of linking other curricular areas to the study of the grade-level

Figure 3.6. Concept-Based Curriculum Planning, Grade 5

Core Concept: Change. **Generalization:** The settlers brought changes to the environment, **Grade:** 5
culture, and people of the West.

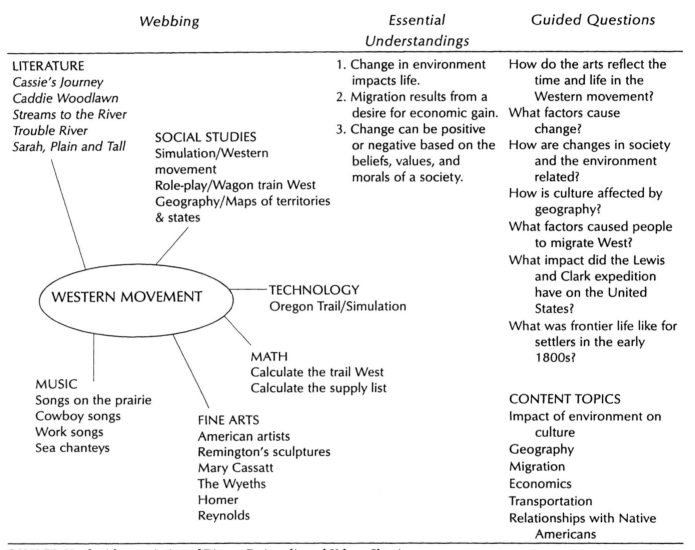

	Webbing	*Essential Understandings*	*Guided Questions*

LITERATURE
Cassie's Journey
Caddie Woodlawn
Streams to the River
Trouble River
Sarah, Plain and Tall

SOCIAL STUDIES
Simulation/Western movement
Role-play/Wagon train West
Geography/Maps of territories & states

WESTERN MOVEMENT

TECHNOLOGY
Oregon Trail/Simulation

MATH
Calculate the trail West
Calculate the supply list

MUSIC
Songs on the prairie
Cowboy songs
Work songs
Sea chanteys

FINE ARTS
American artists
Remington's sculptures
Mary Cassatt
The Wyeths
Homer
Reynolds

1. Change in environment impacts life.
2. Migration results from a desire for economic gain.
3. Change can be positive or negative based on the beliefs, values, and morals of a society.

How do the arts reflect the time and life in the Western movement?
What factors cause change?
How are changes in society and the environment related?
How is culture affected by geography?
What factors caused people to migrate West?
What impact did the Lewis and Clark expedition have on the United States?
What was frontier life like for settlers in the early 1800s?

CONTENT TOPICS
Impact of environment on culture
Geography
Migration
Economics
Transportation
Relationships with Native Americans

SOURCE: Used with permission of Dianne DeAngelis and Yelena Shapiro.

concept. Curricular areas such as Fine Arts and Literature are woven into the conceptual base. Once the process of clearly defining the critical content is decided, along with the student expectancies, coordinating other areas of the curriculum is relatively easy. With carefully laid out essential understandings, guided questions, and student expectancies, the teacher can easily weave in other areas of the curriculum and lay out day-by-day plans. It is only when teachers attempt to do the webbing first that confusion in the planning process occurs (see Figure 3.6).

Figure 3.7. Schoolwide Concept Articulation

Focus Statement: By the end of Walt Disney School's study of culture, all students will (a) take pride in their own culture, and (b) have a respect and appreciation of other cultures.

Grade-Level Concepts

Grade 5	1. The American people then and now are a people of many races, religions, and national origins who live under a common government.
	2. The colonization of America was made up of many cultures.
	3. Geographic location and climate affect one's culture.
Grade 4	1. Culture is made up of various aspects, such as literature, language, music, art, traditions, and so forth.
	2. Native California was composed of many native tribes whose culture and traditions were diverse and directly related to the environment of each tribe.
	3. Diversity, as many of the Native California tribes understood, is something to be valued.
Grade 3	1. People have beliefs that guide their way of life.
	2. People have traditions and ceremonies they pass on to each generation.
	3. People live according to their environment, using the natural resources available to them.
Grade 2	1. Ancestors provide traditions and customs.
	2. Different cultures have different lifestyles, customs, and traditions.
	3. Life in the past and present has both similarities and differences.
Grade 1	1. Each family has its own culture, and each family member is important in his or her own way.
	2. People are alike in some ways and different in others.
	3. Each culture has important people who have made significant contributions to society.
Grade K	1. Culture is the food we eat.
	2. Culture is the special days we celebrate.
	3. Culture is art, music, literature, and clothing.

Step 10: Articulate Grade-Level Concepts in the School

We have felt that it is important to articulate these concepts at all grade levels after teachers have identified the essential understandings at specific grade levels. This articulation builds understanding among grade levels and provides a curriculum map. The "hidden" curriculum becomes a curriculum that is shared and embraced by the total school rather than the "published" curriculum in the curriculum guide, which often is only casually acknowledged.

In addition, we develop an overall focus statement for the schoolwide concept that provides a rationale and direction for the study (see Figure 3.7). For example, the focus statement for the concept Culture is, "As a re-

Figure 3.8. Grade 3 Writing/Content Rubric

	5 Exceptional	4 Fluent	3 Able	2 Developing	1 Emergent
Definition	An EXCEPTIONAL writer is enthusiastic and independent.	A FLUENT writer is independent.	An ABLE writer can write sentences and/or a story with minimal help.	A DEVELOPING writer has limited writing ability.	An EMERGENT writer may use random letters or beginning/ending letters to represent words or pictures.
Mechanics	Writing has minimal errors in capitalization, punctuation, and spelling. Uses varied sentence beginnings.	Creates sentences with few errors in capitalization, punctuation, and spelling.	There are some errors in capitalization, punctuation, and spelling.	Spelling errors and misuse of capitalization, punctuation, and words affect readability.	There is little or no relationship between spelling and words.
Content	Takes risks to explore ideas. Fully answers question. Wide range of examples. Insightful connections to other topics.	Explores ideas with little risk taking. Fully answers question. Multiple examples. Some insightful connections.	Ideas developed in a predictable manner. Addresses the topic. Answers the question. Some examples.	Explores few ideas. Begins to answer questions. May stray from topic. Some information may be incomplete or erroneous.	Does not answer questions in writing. Dictated answer. Answers a different question.
Style	Writes naturally. Lively language with a degree of sophistication. Writes conversationally	Writes naturally with some conversational style. Less sophisticated language.	Writes in a commonplace voice. Writes with simplicity.	Simplistic language. Limited choice of words.	Garbled or confused language. Meager choice of words.
Fluency	Detailed and descriptive writing. Flows naturally; easy to follow thoughts.	Expresses ideas easily. Beginning to use detailed and descriptive language. Shift in thought less fluid.	Able to express ideas. Generally understandable. Straightforward with little description. Coherent.	Writing strays from topic. May be vague or confusing.	Some words and phrases may have been copied. Little or no evidence of fluency or coherence.
Editing	Student edits own writing.	Begins to edit own writing.	Little or no self-editing is evident.	No evidence of self-editing.	No evidence of self-editing.

sult of Walt Disney School's study of Culture, all students will: (1) take pride in their own culture and (2) have a respect and appreciation of other cultures." The essential understandings presented with this focus statement provide a spiral curriculum that addresses a concept like Culture all the way through each grade level, a spiral in that at every level children learn a new dimension of that Big Idea and perfect their own process skills in the exploration.

Step 11: Assess Student Expectancies to Improve Future Curriculum Development

As a part of the planning process for a schoolwide concept, each grade level develops a writing prompt that will measure concept acquisition as well as the skills of the writing process. The prompt is based directly on the concepts developed at each grade level (see Figure 3.8). A rubric or scoring device is developed at grade level to assess both concept acquisition and writing mechanics. The rubric defines what is acceptable concept mastery by assigning a numerical score. Students can score between 1 and 5, with 5 as the highest score. Additional numerical scores are given for writing mechanics and writing fluency. These three scores then provide an assessment of both knowledge and skill.

Completed writing prompts are placed in grade-level portfolios. Three schoolwide concepts and three prompts implemented over the course of a year are developed. The child's portfolio then will have three samples indicating concept mastery and writing skills by the end of the school year. This portfolio is passed to the next grade at the close of the school year. Also, a student technology project is selected by the teacher, one demonstrating the highest level of technology skill during the school concept studies. These projects are also placed in the portfolio.

After scoring grade-level prompts, teachers meet together at the close of the concept studies (fall, winter, and spring) to assess overall student progress at grade level. Teachers use actual scored prompts to determine the level of concept mastery as well as writing fluency and mechanics. Together, teachers determine what concepts will need further development as well as what writing skills will need to be addressed in up-coming instruction. These results are further articulated with the entire staff so that grade levels are aware of the assessments. Such sharing brings an awareness of the skill level at grade levels and serves to focus and challenge teachers collectively. Student technology projects, such as an interactive book, written reports with illustrations, and so on, are also shared to provide an awareness of what is acceptable grade-level progress as well as to challenge teachers with "what is possible with students." Further growth in technology can be stimulated as teachers learn from each other and begin to try new ideas.

4 CHAPTER

The Essential Components of a Quality Technology Plan

Developing a quality plan is a critical element in establishing a strong technology program at your school. This plan reflects the collaborative "oath" of your staff regarding how technology will be used with students and the action steps to be taken. The first page denotes this primary focus with a written mission statement for students. Student expectancies and benchmarks describe how technology will be specifically applied to your concept-based curriculum. The last part of your plan describes networking, hardware and software, staff training, budget, and management issues to support student expectancies.

This plan is a "living" document and reflects the shared belief of a school staff about technology use. Often plans generated by schools do not represent the beliefs of the school staff. Without consensus, any plan is frustrated and will not lead to any long-term changes or improvement. Frustrated plans are those that start with resistance and never change the fabric of the school culture or affect student learning.

Your school staff does not need to know everything about technology to formulate a plan. A technology plan is dynamic and will grow in complexity as your school staff gains in experience and knowledge in working with technology over time. When the staff of Walt Disney School formulated its first plan, we had very limited knowledge of technology use. We simply had a vision for what we wanted for our students, and we knew that using technology would help students improve their writing skills.

Within 2 months of establishing a basic technology plan, California Supplemental Grant Money became available to School Improvement Schools. These funds were just what we needed to begin our technology program. We had already formulated our plans and could easily complete an application and justification for the use of these funds (see Figures 4.1 and 4.2). This was the starting place for our new technology program.

Figure 4.1. School Plan for Consolidated Programs

Burbank Unified School District

WALT DISNEY ELEMENTARY SCHOOL

1220 W. Orange Grove Avenue
Burbank, CA 91506 (818) 558-5385
FAX (818) 558-4664

SCHOOL PLAN FOR CONSOLIDATED PROGRAMS

SUPPLEMENTAL GRANT PLAN
MAY 1990 FOR 1989-1990

INSTRUCTION AREA: English language arts, history/social science, and science

MISSION STATEMENT: Students will use computer technology to apply elements of the writing process to formulate and communicate ideas through the production of illustrated published products in a laboratory setting. Through the use of computers in a laboratory setting and the use of community resources, a meaningful context of today's business world will be provided to all students. Not only will students be learning the basic processes of research and writing, but they will be working cooperatively in groups to integrate these skills in publishing. A laboratory setting will help teachers to personalize instruction and provide greater computer access for students.

CHANGE INITIATIVE:

1. **Related Criterion Areas:** Incorporate the use of computers and integrate the writing process in all curriculum areas as required by the state quality criteria through a publishing and research center linking our six Apple IIe computers with eight new Macintosh SE HD20 computers.

2. **Evidence of What Is:** Inadequate equipment is available in only a few classrooms. Teachers are not trained in the use of computers.

3. **Change Initiative:** Using a computer network in a laboratory and research center, with selected materials and proper training of staff, all students will have access to quality materials and current technology. This computer-based educational program will improve students' skills and better prepare them for the Information Age of their future where computers are indispensable tools for learning and working.

4. **Rationale:** We will address improving student academic achievement in language arts using computers by focusing on communication skills through literature, reading comprehension, research, oral presentations, and written expression including charts, graphs, and illustrations.

Preparing children for the future.

(continued)

Figure 4.1. School Plan for Consolidated Programs *(continued)*

---

5. **Budget:**　Equipment (hardware and software)　　$28,500
　　　　　　　　Teacher inservicing　　　　　　　　$　3,500
　　　　　　　　Improvements　　　　　　　　　　　$　1,320
　　　　　　　　Other books/materials　　　　　　　$　1,306

6. **Persons Responsible:** Classroom teachers, support personnel, principal, computer consultant, county computer consultant.

7. **How Monitored:** Log of classroom use of lab, display of published materials, teacher and principal observation, roster of staff inservice training.

8. **Evaluation:** Compare program with quality criteria, staff and parent observations, and quality of student published work.

The Essential Ingredients of a Quality Plan

Beyond our first Supplemental Grant Plan, we began to determine essential factors for developing a school plan that would express our expectancies for students and specify ingredients necessary for making these student expectations a reality. In addition, we wanted a plan that would be simple, clear, and usable for all staff. After 11 years of experience, we have identified seven essential ingredients of a quality technology plan.

Formulate a Technology Mission Statement Based on Your Students

The first essential ingredient in building a "quality" plan is to formulate a technology mission statement about how your students will use technology. A school must answer the question, "How will technology benefit students and improve their achievement?" All plans must begin here. If a plan begins with what equipment will be purchased, then the school either doesn't have or has lost sight of the reason for technology. Unfortunately, buying equipment is very often the first step most schools take (see Figure 4.3).

A technology mission statement is the *shared belief* of your staff about how technology will be used. It is the focus for the school's technology program. It must reflect what a staff believes about using technology with students. For example, the 1998 Walt Disney School Technology Mission Statement is:

The Disney staff strongly believes that all students must have access to a technology-enhanced curriculum so that they can manage

Figure 4.2. Supplemental Grant Budget

Equipment/Hardware and Software		
Hardware		$26,500
Software		$ 2,000
Improvements		
Electrical	$ 300	
Security	$1,020	$ 1,320
Training		
Substitutes	$1,000	
Teacher Conferences	$2,000	
Administrative Conferences	$ 500	$ 3,500
Other Books/Materials		$ 1,306
TOTAL		**$34,626**

and find information, communicate, and produce meaningful products for living in a global society.

This technology mission statement has grown in sophistication from 1989 when we started. However, our focus is still on improving student writing and communication skills. Over the years, we have expanded our statement from writing and publishing skills to include a broader definition of communication skills: research (including Internet research), organization of information, multimedia presentations, communication with others through electronic mail, and Web publishing of student projects.

Our Technology Mission Statement is further defined in three action statements agreed upon by staff as shown in Figure 4.3. These action statements readily identify the importance of a planned and focused curriculum at Walt Disney School. Achieving the first statement depends on coordinating technology with an organizational structure of teaching concepts where process skills are emphasized. The outcomes of teaching students conceptually are curriculum projects, which demonstrate process skills. Also embedded in these statements is the expectation that students will become competent in applying technology skills to the curriculum (e.g., the basic operation of the computer, keyboarding, software applications, Internet research, publishing, electronic mail, and multimedia). Students will also have participated in projects that are meaningful and demand thinking and preparation. Another important emphasis is that our students, representing 12 languages, will have worked collaboratively and cooperatively in the use of technology. We believe effective working in teams is a skill required by business in a global society and we feel it is our

Figure 4.3. Technology Mission

> **The Disney staff strongly believes that all students must have access to a technology-enhanced curriculum so that they can manage and find information, communicate, and produce meaningful products for living in a global society.**

Therefore:

All students will become competent in using technology as a tool to enhance curriculum projects that support the integration of process skills in oral and written communication, calculations, solving problems, research, organization, and presentation of information.

All students will learn to access and use Internet resources for technology-enhanced curriculum projects cooperatively, ethically, and collaboratively.

All students will have opportunities to produce and share technology-enhanced curriculum projects cooperatively, ethically, and collaboratively.

duty to provide team-working experiences so that children prepare for careers in the 21st century.

Formulate Student Expectancies and Benchmarks from the School Mission Statement

The next level of organization in your technology plan is the development of student expectancies. A Technology Mission Statement is a broad statement, whereas student expectancies help to narrow the focus and provide meaning to the Mission Statement. To develop these statements, your school must answer the question, "How do we want students to specifically use technology?" (see Figure 4.4).

Figure 4.4. Student Expectancies

Student Expectancies
All students at Walt Disney School will:

1. **Apply a variety of software applications to the creation of grade-level curriculum projects in language arts, math, science, history/social science, and fine arts.**

    1.1. Students will develop and apply the language arts skills of listening, reading, writing, and speaking in grade-level technology projects. These projects will also demonstrate the use and development of the writing process (research, prewriting, drafting, editing, revising, and publishing).

    1.2. Students will use technology as a tool to integrate curricular areas in their technology projects.

2. **Access and analyze reference information within curriculum in a variety of media formats using CD-ROM and laser disc media and telecommunications with educational research agencies, and be able to access current information on the World Wide Web.**

    2.1. Students will regularly access Internet resources on the World Wide Web, CD-ROM, and laser disc information for curriculum projects; communicate with educational research agencies to obtain and share current data (e.g., NASA Spacelink, Ask a Geologist, Ask ERIC, Getty Arts Ed Net); and download research data (text, picture, or graphics) for curriculum projects or Web sites by accessing the World Wide Web.

3. **Be provided with opportunities to develop the thinking skills of application, synthesis, analysis, and evaluation through the completion of technology-enhanced curriculum projects.**

    3.1. Students will apply, analyze, and synthesize curricular information in a variety of multimedia formats using text, video, and pictures (e.g., development of slide shows, interactive books, and creation and posting of student Web sites using the Internet).

4. **Collaborate in heterogeneous groupings to share information and access diverse student talents in the production of technology-enhanced curriculum projects.**

    4.1. Students will learn to collaborate and problem solve with other students of diverse cultural backgrounds cooperatively in the creation of technology-enhanced curriculum projects.

As a result of answering this question, our staff developed the expectancies shown in Figure 4.4 for 1998-1999. From these schoolwide expectancies for all students, benchmarks or specific targets were identified for our technology program. Benchmarks serve further to narrow the focus for the use of technology with students and provide teachers with specific and tangible targets. Benchmarks must link with the school's curriculum. Walt Disney School's benchmarks are identified under our expectancies in Figure 4.4.

Establish Grade-Level Expectations From Student Expectancies

The next essential ingredient comes about from establishing Technology Grade-Level Expectations. This step further narrows the focus for a specific group of students at a particular grade level. Often, when schoolwide expectancies have been adopted, actual planning for implementation at a grade level is omitted. There can be no real implementation unless grade-level teachers "own" the expectancies and integrate them within their curricular planning and instructional practice. This is often a missing link in the integration of technology.

In order to create these expectancies, a grade level must ask, "What entry-level and exit technology skills are required at this grade level?" (Figure 4.5). For example, the entry-level skills for kindergarten at Walt Disney School include basic instruction in computer use such as start-up, use of the mouse, recognizing icons and symbols, opening/closing files, opening applications, and saving files. These entry-level skills allow kindergarten students to begin writing basic words and using a drawing tool to create pictures and to recognize letters and numbers with symbols. A set of exit technology skills for kindergarten includes reading, writing, and recording words for a slide show about their study of the garden for the curricular concept Change.

When all grade levels have established entry-level and exit skills for students, the skills are articulated at every grade level and adjusted so that skills and expectations are sequential and increase in complexity. These skills are adjusted each year as the technology program develops. Entry-level and exit skills at each grade level help to build a continuum of skills that will result in students eventually exiting from the school, meeting the global student expectancies originally established.

Select Hardware and Software Based on Student Expectancies

Student expectancies for technology must guide the selections for hardware and software purchase. Unfortunately, in some schools equipment is purchased with little thought as to how students will use it. These

Figure 4.5. Grade-Level Expectancies

Grade-Level Expectancies

Kindergarten–2nd Grade

Disney students will be introduced to a broad range of technology experiences. The introduction should include instruction in basic computer use such as start-up, opening/closing files and applications, disk management, and appropriate computer care. Students will learn how to explore or browse through various grade-level-appropriate programs and Internet Web sites. Also, students will create documents based upon curricular activities and objectives that include pictures and words, and begin to edit, format, and publish their work. Computer presentations of student work will be enhanced by adding voice narrations in computer-generated slide shows.

3rd–5th Grade

Disney students will work toward proficiency of grade-level expectancies. Students will create presentations, including desktop publishing and hypermedia presentations, to enhance their curricular studies in all areas. Increased proficiency of keyboarding will be expected. Presentations will include carefully selected materials, including scanned and digital camera images, along with CD-ROM, laser disc, and Internet resources. Students will learn communication skills by using a computer, VCR, video scan converter, and video capture tools to create original video presentations that reflect an understanding of curricular objectives. Students will expand their learning community by creating their own Web sites reflecting curricular study, sharing their projects with people across the globe, and researching information using the World Wide Web.

technology purchasing decisions often reside in the hands of small committees with neither a plan nor the total inclusion of staff. As a result, money is wasted and technology use remains in the hands of a few staff interested in technology rather than becoming a powerful tool in the hands of all students and teachers. Hardware and software must be purchased based on what we want students to do.

Our first plan for students in 1989 was to obtain computer hardware and software to improve student writing in the core curriculum. Specifically, we wanted students to use word processing and publishing within the curriculum. Based on that student expectancy, we purchased: eight Macintosh SE 20s, one of which was used as a dedicated file server; a scanner; a modem; and a laser printer. The software we purchased included Microsoft Works, a basic word processing program; PageMaker for publishing; and file server software. These purchases, along with the decision to create a lab to provide maximum access for all students, were directly related to our student expectancies.

Today, we are still purchasing equipment based on what we want students to do. In 1998 our emphasis was on continuing to improve communication skills, but the focus had expanded to include multimedia presentations, development of interactive books, Internet research, development of Web sites, communication through e-mail, and so on. These projects and skills demand the use of technology. With this expanding focus, there is still a greater need for hardware and more sophisticated software programs as well as the networking infrastructure to support a growing local area network (LAN). There is also a greater demand to upgrade memory requirements on machines, obtain powerful file servers, purchase current software, expand networking, and more. Our number one consideration for hardware purchase is buying workstations for students in order to provide more student access to technology tools. We are now planning for two computer labs as well as from three to six computers per classroom, until every student has access to a computer.

Create Stages of Integration

In order to plan for hardware and software purchases in an organized and systematic fashion, we constructed a page called the "Stages of Integration" in our technology plan that has assisted us in linking student expectancies with hardware and software purchases (see Figure 4.6). With this graphic organizer, we began by first listing our student expectancies. Based on these expectancies, we identified the technology skills we wanted to develop. These skills have been previously planned and identified by grade levels. With these two categories completed, we determined what hardware and software will be selected in priority order. The Stages of Integration represents a present plan, a future plan, and a past plan. The past plan always provides us with a record of what we have accomplished, and the future projection helps us to focus our priorities beyond where we are each year. This special planning tool assists us in creating more depth in our technology program as well as to maintain a constant focus on improving our technology program.

Establish a Budget Based on Student Expectancies

Another mistake often made by schools is allowing the budget to determine the kind of technology program that will exist. When a school leadership team makes this crucial mistake, its technology program will always be limited by the budget. Thus the technology program will not go forward. Planning must always precede establishing a budget. The first

Figure 4.6. Stages of Integration: Walt Disney School

Stages of Integration: Walt Disney School

Software and Hardware	Technology Skills	Student Expectancies

One Computer Lab
 	
(Consisting of 16 networked Macintosh workstations connected to a file server using local talk and 8 Apple IIe computers)
 	
Other Resources
 	
Printers (2 image writers, 1 laser)
Scanner   Cable TV
TV & VCR   Laser disc players
PageMaker   Microsoft Works
Modem
	Introduction to
	  Basic computer skills
	  Appropriate typing skills
	  Word processing
	  Illustrations & graphics
	  Desktop publishing
	
	Browsing Resources
	  Laser discs
	
	Introduction to
	  Slide shows
	  Hypermedia presentations
		Students will
		  Demonstrate the writing process within the core curriculum by using word processing and desktop publishing
		  Access reference information using laser discs and National Geographic telecommunications projects.

One Computer Lab
 	
(Consisting of 30 networked Macintosh workstations connected to a workgroup server 7350 using Ethernet)
 	
Computers in the Classroom
 	
(31 Macintosh workstations and 3 laser printers connected to the 10 M/s school LAN through Ethernet)
 	
Library Media Center
 	
Computerized catalog/circulation system
 	
Other Resources
 	
Digital camera   Video network
Sonic network   CD-ROMs
  access
Color scanner   Network mail
3 Modems   Internet access
Variety of   Cisco router
  software
	Mastery of
	  Basic computer skills
	  Keyboarding skills
	  Word processing
	  Illustrations & graphics
	  Desktop publishing
	  Slide shows
	  Hypermedia presentations
	  HTML publishing
	
	Browsing Resources
	  Multimedia CDs & laser discs
	  Library resources
	  Internet resources
	  Cable in the Classroom videos
		Students will
		  Apply applications to core curriculum projects.
		  Access and analyze reference information in a variety of media formats.
		  Extend critical thinking, problem-solving, and decision-making skills through application.
		  Collaborate in heterogeneous groupings to access student talents for creation of enhanced curriculum projects.
		  Work ethically, independently, and collaboratively with a diverse and changing population within the school.

(continued)

Figure 4.6. Stages of Integration: Walt Disney School *(continued)*

Stages of Integration: Walt Disney School (continued)

Software and Hardware	Technology Skills	Student Expectancies
Multiple Computer Labs (Connected to the 100 M/s Disney local area network [labs, research library, and classrooms]) **3-6 Computers** **in Each classroom** (Connected to the 100 M/s & switched hubs to Disney LAN and the district's wide-area network) **Other Resources** Satellite TV Communications Network mail Direct Internet access G3 File Server and back-up storage Video communications	**Mastery of** Basic computer skills Productivity applications Hypermedia presentations Video presentations Internet navigation **Browsing Resources** Multimedia CDs & laser discs Library resources Internet resources **Telecommunications** Information exchange Collaborative documents	**Students will** Create and maintain a video portfolio of curricular activities from Kindergarten through 5th grade. Integrate applications and resources to produce presentations. Create presentations in multiple formats. Access, analyze, organize, and communicate reference information in a variety of formats. Work ethically, independently, and collaboratively with a diverse and changing population across the school, state, national, and international boundaries.

place to start with establishing a budget is to revisit your student expectancies. What is the "vision" for using technology with your students? It is to be hoped that this question has already been answered in the previous planning steps. However, if the vision for your technology program based on student expectancies is not clear in the minds of school staff, the budget cannot be executed effectively, regardless of how much money you have or don't have. Wise choices for hardware and software purchases will always be dictated by what you want for your students.

A key principle for all schools in planning a budget is to match hardware and software purchases with student expectancies in a priority ranking. The Stages of Integration page in our technology plan (refer back to Figure 4.6) very quickly helps us determine a priority for purchases. This planning page also helps to keep our staff on track with what we have purchased as well as what we intend to purchase (see Figure 4.7).

Our budget page in our plan is based on our vision for students first and our existing resources second. Although we have allocated limited existing resources, our budget page reflects the priorities for the future. A large portion of our budget is for adding workstations because we want ALL students increasingly to use technology tools for their work. A second

Figure 4.7. Technology Budget

> Mission Statement: The Disney staff strongly believes that all students must have access to a technology-enhanced curriculum so that they can manage and find information, communicate, and produce meaningful products for living in a global society.

Hardware

8 G3 Workstations	$16,120
2 HP DeskJet Ethernet Color Printers	$ 1,275
4 HP DeskJet Color Printers	$ 1,078
2 HP Printer Servers	$ 503
2 Netgear 16 Port 10 Base-T Hubs	$ 346
4 Asante 10 Base-T Hubs	$ 217
1 G3 333 MHz File Server	$ 4,480
15 64 Mg Dimms/Memory for Workstations/File Server	$ 1,950
	$25,969

Software

ClarisWorks 5.0	$ 1,140
Caspr Library Software	$ 233
Caspr Library Maintenance Agreement	$ 395
Norton AntiVirus	$ 450
PageMill 3.0	$ 750
Retrospect Express	$ 50
ANAT (Apple Network Administrator Tool Kit)	$ 1,200
AppleShare	$ 1,200
	$ 5,418

Maintenance

Repairs	$ 1,500
Cables	$ 450
Cartridges (color)	$ 750
Cartridges (b/w)	$ 830
Mouse Replacement	$ 500
Cleaning Supplies	$ 150
	$ 4,180

Staff training	**$ 2,500**
GRAND TOTAL	**$38,067**

category of emphasis in our budget is teacher training because, in order to fulfill our vision for students, teachers must be able to conduct learning in a technology classroom. All teachers are trained in various aspects of technology, such as new application and management software, on a regular basis. A third category of emphasis in our budget is technology maintenance. This category consists of software (including anti-virus, network, and application software), memory upgrades for workstations, hardware (including Ethernet hubs, routers, or file servers), cabling, repairs, and cleaning.

Empower (Train) Teachers to Use Technology With the Curriculum

Before students can use technology effectively with the curriculum, all teachers at the site must be empowered through training to use technology. Training all teachers is more effective than designating or hiring "a computer teacher" for classrooms. Teachers who are trained in basic technology skills, specific applications, and computer lab management can creatively use technology tools and apply these skills to the curriculum. A designated computer teacher for all classrooms will not be able to link technology skills creatively to the curriculum because that teacher would see those students for only one part of the day. Then too, computer time becomes a departmentalized event once per week rather than being integrated with all of the instruction in the classroom (Figure 4.8).

At Walt Disney School, all teachers are trained to become competent in using the hardware, software, and multimedia resources available within the core curriculum. Teachers are trained in strategies that integrate technology with curriculum at each grade level. Students are instructed by teachers in basic technology skills (keyboarding, word processing, and publishing) to enhance curriculum projects. Teachers also train students to use multimedia applications such as HyperStudio, Action, and Kid Pix Slide Show to integrate video, speaking, reading, and writing skills. Internet research, reporting, and posting of Web pages are additional skills that students learn from teachers. These activities with students would not happen if teachers were not trained.

Our two on-site technology specialists (who are also teachers in the regular classroom) oversee the school's technology plan and lead staff technology training. Training is planned and conducted by the specialists throughout the year in a variety of formats, including peer coaching, after-school training, informal collaboration, hands-on workshops, site visitations, and summer training. These specialists also train teachers to solve problems that may come about in the computer lab.

Organize a Management Team to Oversee the Technology Program

One of the most overlooked areas of a technology plan is the ongoing management of the technology environment at the school. With technol-

Figure 4.8. Teacher Training Focus

Teacher Training Focus

Teachers will become competent in using hardware, software, and multimedia resources available within the core curriculum. All teachers will receive extensive training in strategies integrating technology with curriculum at each grade level.

Teachers will be empowered to use technology to:

Instruct students in basic technology skills as a tool for enhancing grade-level projects.

Use technology such as multimedia applications, Internet resources, electronic communications, CD-ROMs, VCRs, and laser discs to enhance instruction in the core curriculum.

Use electronic mail to communicate with other teachers within the school as well as resource specialists in other schools and across the world.

Use technology to generate additional instructional resources and help manage required record keeping.

On-site training will be provided during the year through (a) peer coaching on released days, (b) after-school training, (c) informal collaboration, (d) hands-on workshops, (e) site visitations, (f) use of Powerbook checkout, and (g) regular summer training for all staff members to keep them updated on changing technology issues.

Two site technology specialists will oversee Disney's technology, lead staff technology committee meetings and trainings, and relay any concerns to the district technology coordinator.

ogy, any number of problems can and will occur. The first and most important task of management is the creation of a schedule for the greatest student access (especially with a computer lab or a limited number of computers). Schools must then deal with ongoing issues of printing problems, network problems, system software corruption, and so on. Schools must create and train a management team to deal with these issues (Figure 4.9).

The technology management team is also responsible for the security of the technology equipment and the software, and for preventing inap-

Figure 4.9. Technology Management

Technology Management

Security   Computers are secured in the lab by an alarm system. A "staff watch" system is used to secure the computers in the lab as well as those in the classrooms.

A firewall computer located at the City of Burbank is used to limit access to inappropriate URL sites on the Internet.

At Ease for Workgroups prevents users from illegally copying software from workstations.

Scheduling   Grades K-2 students are scheduled a minimum of 1.5 hours per week. Grades 3-5 students are scheduled 3 hours per week.

Maintenance   A maintenance team of site technology specialists and the principal oversee networking, software installations, computer set-up, and emergency response.

propriate Internet access. Computers and other technology equipment are secured through an alarm system. Along with the alarm system, a staff "watch" system is in place, with the management team checking every day that the school is secure. Software and files are secured through a software management program on the file server. All student files are backed up every night through an automated system. Software copies and licenses are secured in a locked closet. Internet access to inappropriate sites is screened by a "firewall" computer located at the city of Burbank, our Internet source provider. The firewall screens Internet addresses and prevents access to inappropriate sites on the World Wide Web.

These and other management issues, including planning and committee meetings, are organized by the management team at Walt Disney School. This team consists of the site technology specialists and the principal. These on-site specialists help teachers solve problems in the computer lab as well as in the classrooms. When a severe problem arises, the principal or these specialists assist teachers either through arranging class coverage during the day or by meeting with teachers during recess, lunch, or after school. These specialists also assist in the general maintenance of the computers: loading software, setting up programs, changing printer cartridges, using utilities to fix system problems, and changing out system software, among other tasks. Specialists also train teachers in the general maintenance issues connected with working in the computer lab.

Figure 4.10. Program Evaluation

Program Evaluation

Students will create video portfolios, published technology-enhanced curriculum projects (e.g., student newspapers, interactive books), and Web sites to demonstrate their use of technology with curriculum.

Students will increasingly use more advanced applications (e.g., PageMaker, HyperStudio, PageMill) and demonstrate greater technology skill in curriculum projects through various technologies. A scoring rubric will be used to assess technology skills at all grade levels.

Student products will show improvement in their demonstration of understanding concepts in core curriculum as measured by a scoring rubric for curriculum. Students will also be evaluated through exit skills as identified in the technology continuum.

Teachers will assist students in applying technology skills gained from training in the computer lab and classrooms to the curriculum as shown by student work samples.

Teacher and parent surveys will provide feedback for the present and future instructional program using technology.

Evaluate Technology Program Based on Student Expectancies

The effectiveness of a technology program must be measured by student achievement of grade-level expectancies. Students are evaluated through published or videotaped technology-enhanced curriculum projects, including reports, stories, newspapers, interactive books, or Web pages that demonstrate their use of technology. Each project is evaluated and scored through the use of a rubric that measures technology skill at that grade level. Grade-level entry and exit technology skills provide an additional comparison for evaluating student skill. Teachers monitor the growth of technology skills through projects placed in schoolwide portfolios during the year (Figure 4.10).

In addition, student technology projects are evaluated for demonstrating understanding of curricular concepts within the California frameworks. This understanding of curricular concepts is measured through grade-level scoring rubrics that are standardized in the Burbank Unified School District.

Student expectancies are also measured by observing students working with technology as they complete curricular projects and other work. Teachers keep anecdotal records of students working in teams and working independently on projects. These observations form another level of evaluation of students working collaboratively and cooperatively.

Other measures we use for evaluating the technology program include teacher and parent surveys that provide feedback for technology planning. Survey findings are applied to revisions of student expectancies and grade-level exit skills. In addition, teacher training is updated based on technology changes and developing teacher expertise. Overall, evaluation provides us with a means of continuous improvement to the technology program and the fulfillment of the technology mission for the school.

CHAPTER 5

Using Grade-Level Technology Skills to Enhance the Curriculum

··

Very often, technology and the skills associated with it, or both, are seen as a separate curriculum, something that stands alone, something our students must learn to get along in the world today or tomorrow. But our experiences at Disney have shown us that technology is not a curriculum in and of itself. Primarily, requisite skills for technology are process skills that include reading, writing, listening, speaking, thinking, and computing, and what's more, they are integrated forms of reading, writing, speaking, thinking, listening, and computing. These process skills differ significantly from content skills in that they develop internally within each student.

When technology skills are learned in concert with other process skills and then applied to the integrated curriculum, the level of student thinking is immediately elevated. For example, when kindergarten students create sound/symbol associations using Kid Pix in the creation of letters, words, numbers, and pictures, they are using language arts skills as well as the technology skills of manipulating the mouse, selecting letters/numbers, drawing pictures, or recording their voice into the computer. Thus both language arts process skills as well as technology skills in combination are being taught. Students are provided an opportunity to practice both sets of process skills in an integrated context through using technology.

Technology skills apply and extend other process skills to a very high level. Technology actually integrates reading, writing, speaking, and thinking with the skills built into a single software application, for example, HyperStudio. Think about all of the steps involved in using basic word processing on the computer. In order to word process and publish effectively, a student must not only be able to read, write, and speak but also able to type, access software commands from menus, edit by manipulating the mouse, import or draw graphics, and print a document. Technology takes the common tasks that have been traditionally done with paper and pencil and places them in a highly integrated creative format. In this integrated format, the thinking level of students is elevated. The traditional process skills approached with paper and pencil alone will not have the same effect.

Integrating language arts process skills and technology skills with a concept-based curriculum elevates student thinking and assists the development of essential understandings to a high level. When these skills interact with the content of an integrated curriculum, student products show great depth of understanding and applied thinking. In addition, the mutual interdependence of language arts skills and technology skills provides students much practice in the application of these skills to the concepts under study.

Integrating Technology Skills
With the Curriculum

The organization of the curriculum at grade level determines how technology skills will be used. Teachers decide in preliminary planning how technology will enhance certain projects. These projects are aligned with student expectancies. Specific technologies for use with students are chosen based on the level of technology training of the teacher. In developing writing for technology enhancement, one first-grade teacher, using the writing process with her students, wrote about the artist, Matisse. After students edited their final drafts with their teacher in the classroom (see Figure 5.1), the final drafts were taken into the computer lab to be typed (Figure 5.2) and then illustrated using SuperPrint (Figure 5.3).

One of the fourth-grade teachers worked with students to develop personified characters within the core concept Interdependence using the writing process (Figure 5.4). When the stories are written and edited, the teacher then works with students to develop storyboards (Figures 5.5 and 5.6). Students decide how their stories will be divided and illustrated with pictures. Students draw illustrations for their stories. Pictures are then scanned into the computer and imported into HyperStudio. HyperStudio is a multimedia software program that enables students to organize text, pictures, video, and voice in sequential frames (Figures 5.7 and 5.8). These pictures are colored and illustrated in the HyperStudio program. Text is then typed in each HyperStudio card that will fit with each illustrated picture. Students can further enhance their stories by recording their voice as they read their story. Now what traditionally was a paper-and-pencil assignment has dramatically changed into a highly integrated multimedia project utilizing all the language arts process skills along with a layer of integrated technology skills. Immediately, the level of thinking of this technology-enhanced writing activity has been elevated from a traditional writing task.

Figure 5.1. Henri Matisse

Henri Matisse

When Matisse was very sick the nuns took good care of him. The nuns asked him if he wanted to help build the chapel and he said yes, But when he got there, he took over. He was born in France on December 31, 1869. He died of a heart attack while in his daughter arms at the age of 84. When he was young he wasn't interested in art and his father wanted him to be a lawyer or work in a grocery store. He has three chrilden, two boys from his wife and one girl from someone else. When he was twenty, he was sick and he was very bored so his mom got him a paint box. He found out that he likes to paint so he asked his father if he can be a artist an his father said no. He was very poor so his wife had to work at a hat store and model for Matisse and take care of his chrilden. The Jazz is a book where Matisse has his cut out serie in it. He is one of the founders of wild beast style where you use lots of bright colors.

BY Marcus Lopez May 18, 1999

Figure 5.2. Henri Matisse

When Matisse was very sick then the nuns took good care of him. The nuns asked him if he wanted to help build the chapel and he said yes. But when he got there, he took over. He was born in France on December 31, 1869. He died of a heart attack while in his daughter arms at the age of 84. When he was young he wasn't interested in art and his father wanted him to be a lawyer or work in a grocery store. He has three children, two boys from his wife and one girl from someone else. When he was twenty, he was sick and his mom got him a paint box. He found out that he liked to paint so he asked his father if he could be an artist and his father said no. He was very poor so his wife had to work at a hat store and model for him and take care of his children. The Jazz is a book where Matisse has his cut out series in it. He is one of the founders of wild beast style where you use lots of bright colors.

By Marcus Lopez   May 18, 1999

Figure 5.3. The Night Dance

Articulating Technology Skills Grades K-5

In order to articulate the process skills of technology across all grade levels at Walt Disney School, teachers identified the developmental technology skills that were important to each grade level. Entry-level skills or those technology skills that students should start with were identified for each grade level at the beginning of the school year. Exit-level skills that students should master by the end of the school year were also identified (Figure 5.9). A continuum for each grade level was thus established by compiling information from each grade-level team. This continuum was then shared with all teachers and at all grade levels for refinement and adjustment.

Curriculum projects that integrate technology skills were developed from teacher planning. These projects were developed from our three schoolwide core concepts (Interdependence, Culture, Change), using grade-level curricula. Teachers identify grade-level concepts and form generalizations. From these generalizations, essential understandings are established, along with guided questions to direct instruction. Student expectancies directly based on essential understandings were planned, as were specific process skills that interact with the curriculum. These curricular projects were grounded in the entry-level and exiting skills across the school year.

Figure 5.4. Personified Character

Personified Character

By Mary Ann Yap

Once there lived two nice supplies that were very best friends for a long time. Parker W. Paper was a white, flat and friendly piece of paper. Penny R. Pencil was a hard, smart, skinny and pretty ordinary pencil. Both of them had a tiring problem. Parker and Penny needed a vacation from their jobs.

Parker and Penny walked very happily to the ticket counter of the Burbank Airport. Parker took out $1.00 and Penny took out $4.00, and got ready to pay. Both of them gladly put their money on the counter. A sort of stewardess gently said: "I'm so very sorry. We're *all* sold out." So Parker and Penny rudely took their money and angrily walked away.

After they went to Burbank Airport, they were hungry and tired, so they bought some food at Yummy the fast food restaurant. So, Parker and Penny went to another airport out of town. They went to the Sacramento Airport, and were going to buy tickets to go to the Bahamas. They were just getting ready, but they hardly had a penny. So they sadly walked away.

Penny's friend, Polly G. Paper-weight won *2* tickets to the Bahamas in a contest. Polly couldn't go because if she went to the Bahamas, the papers would fly away. So, Polly politely gave her tickets to Penny and Parker, who happily flew to the Bahamas.

Figure 5.5.

Figure 5.6a.   **Figure 5.6b.**

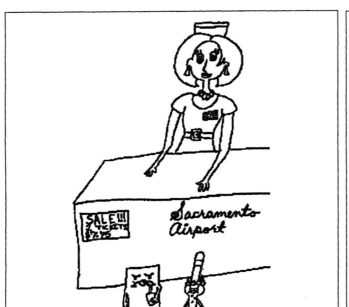

Based on the curriculum projects, software containing specific technology skills was identified. The software inherently had to have specific technology skills that would integrate well with the curriculum and allow students to use them creatively. ClarisWorks, with word processing, formatting, publishing, and drawing tools, fit well with applying the writing process with curriculum. ClarisWorks is an "open-ended" program in that

Figure 5.7.

Figure 5.8a.

Figure 5.8b.

After they went to the Burbank Airport , they were hungry and tired, and so they bought some food at Yummy the fast food resturant. So, Parker and Penny went to another airport out of town. They went to the Sacramento Airport , and were going to buy tickets to go to the Baha mas . They were just getting ready, but they

Where they sun-bathed happily together to the sound of banjos

it can be used for any curriculum project. A tutorial program, such as Math Rabbit, does not have specific technology skills that students can creatively apply to the curriculum. There is only one pathway to a result. The software programs also had to be developmentally appropriate for specific grade levels. For kindergarten, Kid Pix was chosen, as compared to the more complex HyperStudio or PageMaker for the fifth grade. Finally, software programs with specific skills that students could apply to the curriculum were selected only after planning and student expectancies were established.

Kindergarten

Since students are at the beginning stages of their school experience, entry-level technology skills begin with use of the mouse, logging on and opening files, and selecting a software program. The next set of skills includes opening/exiting programs; recognizing icons and symbols; using alphabet tools for writing names, words, and simple sentences; using drawing tools to create pictures; and recording voices. These skills interface with basic language arts skills that are also being developed in kindergarten, such as letter-sound relationships in phonemic awareness; forming basic words and sentences in speaking; decoding letters, words, and simple sentences; and writing letters and words in simple sentences with pictures to illustrate.

Technology-enhanced curriculum projects based on curricular planning for kindergarten at the beginning of the year include typing names,

Figure 5.9. Exit-Level Skills

Grade	Exit-Level Skills
Grade 5	Upload projects to a Web server. Construct a Web site. Prepare and deliver a technology presentation to an audience. Publish a newspaper using text boxes, formatting, graphics, text wrap, and photos. Access information through the Internet or electronic encyclopedia. Animate and record voice, text, and images for a multimedia project. Edit for spelling, punctuation, and grammar. Design and format a document. Word process using a variety of software tools. Keyboard 20 words per minute.
Grade 4	Animate, record voice and images to HyperStudio. Publish a newsletter in Classroom Publisher. Insert images from the digital camera into written materials. Access Web sites associated with curriculum research. Prepare a basic report in HyperStudio and present to an audience. Edit regularly for spelling, punctuation, spacing, centering, indenting, capitalization, and grammar. Wrap text around graphic images. Take notes and outline from the electronic encyclopedia and the Internet. Word process a 2-page research report. Keyboard 10 words per minute.
Grade 3	Present a simple multimedia story to an audience. Publish a story with illustrations using HyperStudio. Outline research information. Import illustrations into HyperStudio; storyboard text from a written fable. Find information on the Internet and electronic encyclopedia. Edit for spelling, punctuation, spacing, centering, indenting, capitalization, and grammar. Word process simple research reports and outlines. Import images from the Internet into reports. Format graphic images. Type with both hands and up to 10 words per minute.
Grade 2	Publish a simple newsletter. Begin locating Internet addresses. Design a newsletter using a title, text boxes, and creating or pasting graphics. Edit text for proper indentation, spacing, centering, correct spelling, and punctuation. Type a friendly letter with a greeting, salutation, body, and ending. Format narratives, stories, and diagrams using font changes, centering, and labeling. Use chooser to select printer. Type narratives and stories. Use art tools to create a diagram with labeling. Use keyboard with left- and right-hand orientation.

Figure 5.9. Exit-Level Skills *(continued)*

Grade	Exit-Level Skills
Grade 1	Sequence and illustrate stories using a slide show. Edit stories for capitalization, spelling, and punctuation. Record their voices reading stories. Break stories into beginning, middle, and end. Write and type stories of three or more sentences. Use tools in Kid Pix and SuperPrint. Read typed simple sentences. Copy simple sentences. Practice finding letters and symbols on keyboard.
Kindergarten	Record voice into the computer. Illustrate words and generate sentences with pictures. Type letters, words; copy simple sentences. Draw pictures using art tools. Type a name using keyboard. Log on; open files. Select software program. Save work. Enter and exit programs. Use mouse.

letters, and numbers using Kid Pix. Kindergarten students start with writing their names and drawing pictures based on the current curriculum study (Figure 5.10). Students then progress to writing basic words and illustrating those words with pictures (Figure 5.11). Math skills are reinforced by number/symbol relationships as students represent numbers with objects much the same as using manipulatives in the classroom. At

Figure 5.10.

Figure 5.11.

Hanna

G is for grass, Godzilla, and glasses.

the end of the year, kindergarten students are able to read and write simple sentences.

During May of each year, kindergarten students complete a project on the garden for the core concept Change. Students explore how changes occur in plants and animals. They participate in growing their own garden and watch the metamorphosis of a silkworm. Technology is used to enhance this concept as students illustrate the phases of metamorphosis of the silk worm (Figure 5.12). Students also use the art tools to create a garden and label its parts (Figure 5.13).

By the end of the year, kindergarten students will:

- Use the mouse
- Log on
- Open files
- Select a software program
- Enter and exit programs
- Save work
- Type a name
- Type letters, words, and simple sentences
- Draw pictures using art tools
- Illustrate words and sentences with pictures
- Record their voices into the computer

Figure 5.12.

The egg is little

The caterpillar is litrle

He makes a cocoon

The butterfly is born

Letty

Grade 1

With introductory technology experiences in kindergarten, students enter Grade 1 with the ability to use the mouse; log onto the file server; open the Kid Pix program; use the keyboard to write names, simple words, or sentences; and use basic art tools for drawing pictures. Students have extreme familiarity with Kid Pix as a beginning program as well as with the software management program At Ease for accessing files and software programs. Students also have familiarity with basic computer care in the use of the mouse and the keyboard.

In Grade 1, students begin basic word processing with Kid Pix and SuperPrint. Students begin by copying a sentence or short paragraph using the keyboard. Students practice finding letters for words on the keyboard. Classroom writing of simple sentences with capitalization and basic punctuation is prepared in the classroom and brought to the computer lab for typing and illustrating (Figure 5.14).

As students become familiar with how stories work, they begin to generate their own stories. The children move from single sentences (Figure 5.15) to sentences linked together into short stories, narrative descriptions (Figure 5.16), and poems (Figure 5.17). Students work on left-to-right orientation, spacing, tracking, capitalization, and periods. The writing is enhanced by student drawings illustrating events in the stories using Super-Print. SuperPrint is a program that combines word processing tools with art tools to create posters, cards, and banners. We've found that the skills

Figure 5.13.

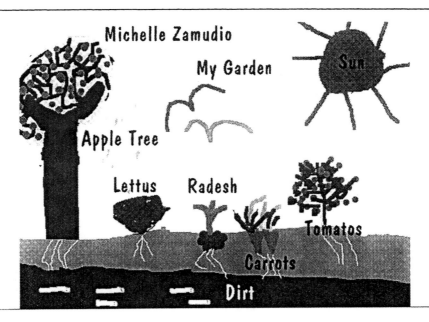

of story retelling and editing built into technology reinforce comprehension and the reading strategies students use to decode and make sense of text.

In January of the school year, students are introduced to multimedia using the slide show portion of Kid Pix. Students learn to sequence parts of a story and illustrate each section. The slide show enables students to tell their stories and record their voices. One first-grade classroom during fall 1998 created a class slide show in which each student drew a picture of him- or herself and recorded his or her voice. This program was shared with parents in the classroom during Back-to-School Night. These parents, as most Disney parents, are appreciative of the work their child produces using the computer. The previous figures are examples of cards created by for the Grade 1 slide show program.

Curriculum projects based on theme planning for Grade 1 include a friendship poster for Interdependence and greeting cards to parents. For the core concept Culture, students wrote stories about the culture they studied and illustrated the stories with pictures. With the core concept Change, students used SuperPrint to write a class book about their visit to a farm.

Students at the end of Grade 1 will have added many technology skills to those learned in kindergarten. These students will exit Grade 1 having learned the following skills:

- Practice finding letters and symbols on the keyboard
- Demonstrate competence in using tools within Kid Pix and Super-Print

Figure 5.14.

- Copy simple sentences
- Compose and type simple sentences
- Read their typed simple sentences
- Write and type stories of three or more sentences
- Break up their stories into beginning, middle, and end
- Sequence and illustrate their stories using a slide show
- Edit stories for capitalization, spelling, and periods
- Record their voices reading their stories

Figure 5.15.

Figure 5.16.

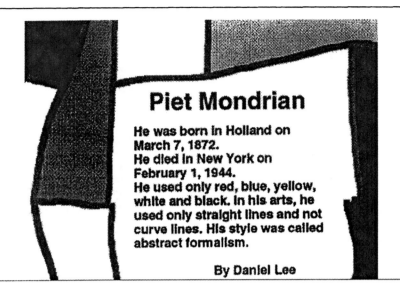

Grade 2

Entry-level technology skills for Grade 2 that are essential for students include:

- Finding their name and file
- Using the keyboard and mouse
- Accessing, saving, and printing documents
- Opening and closing programs

Figure 5.17.

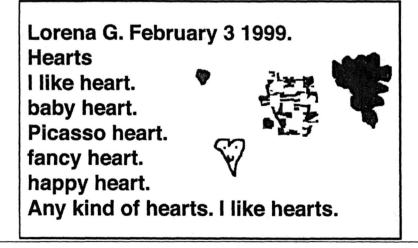

Figure 5.18.

Synjin   Hipolito   Oct.14,1998

MY   FAVORITE   FOOD

My favorite food is crab. I like it because it's soft, good, and sweet. I like it with rice and soy sauce. Also I like spam too! I like it because it's tasty and so, so good. I like it with rice and any kind of sauce. Food is so good!

- Accessing tools for drawing
- Editing work for capitals, spacing, and periods

In addition, students must be able to write their names and type simple sentences by recognizing letters on the keyboard. Familiarity with the tools and use of both SuperPrint and Kid Pix software programs will assist in the next level of skills.

In Grade 2, students continue growth in word processing and creating graphics. Proper left/right orientation with hands on the keyboard is taught. Students continue to work with narratives created in the classroom from the curriculum. However, writing becomes more complex as students use vocabulary from science and history/social science curricula along with priority spelling words to construct paragraphs based on a specific topic. Editing skills, including correcting spelling, correcting spacing errors, centering text, changing font types and sizes, as well as checking for grammatical understanding, are emphasized throughout the year. Additional narratives include the writing of letters, including a letter's opening, salutation, body, and closing. For example, students wrote about their favorite food as a part of their study of Culture (Figure 5.18).

Our students not only write more complex stories and narratives but also label and diagram illustrations associated with science and history/social science. In the core concept Change, students diagram an insect's life cycle; in the core concept Culture, they diagram a volcano using the vocabulary associated with the concepts identified in rocks, minerals, and soil (Figure 5.19). These illustrations build meaning from vocabulary and provide opportunities for students to present orally the concepts learned.

During the last portion of the school year, students are introduced to publishing a basic newsletter using the software program Classroom Pub-

Figure 5.19.

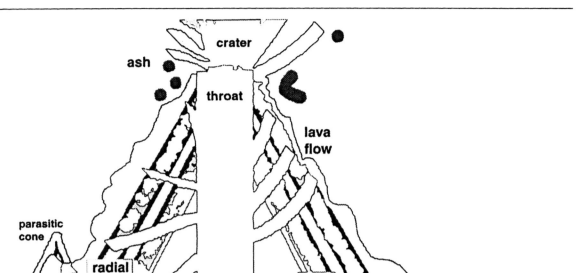

lisher. Students complete an "insect newsletter" based on the concept Change. Technology skills that students acquire include:

- Creating, moving, and altering the font and type sizes in text boxes
- Importing/pasting graphics
- Managing overall design and presentation features
- Selecting printing options

To prepare for building the newsletter in the computer lab, students study basic concepts relating to life cycles as outlined by grade-level curricula under the concept Change. Students gather information from the conceptual generalization, "All organisms have life cycles" using a science investigation of soil (Figure 5.20). Students bring the graphic organizer to the computer lab where technology skills related to publishing are applied. As a result, students gain an understanding of life cycles as well as demonstrate that knowledge through technology skills.

By the end of Grade 2, students have added a significant layer of technology skills to their curriculum studies. Projects are more sophisticated as students are demonstrating understanding of curriculum through polished paragraphs and then formatting their work for publishing. Students will exit Grade 2 with the following technology skills:

Figure 5.20.

What's In Dirt?

I looked at dirt. I saw two
earthworms, roly-polys, ants and bugs
I also saw live plants and dead plants.
There were rotten leaves and old
roots. There were rocks. I was
surprised to see a worm laying eggs.

- Using the keyboard with left- and right-hand orientation
- Using the "chooser" to select a different printer
- Typing narratives and stories
- Using art tools to create a diagram with labeling
- Formatting narratives, stories, and diagrams using font changes, centering, and labeling
- Editing text for proper indentation, correct spacing, centering, use of mouse to correct spelling, and punctuation
- Typing a friendly letter with a greeting, salutation, body, and ending
- Creating introductory design of a newsletter using a title, text boxes, and creating or pasting graphics
- Publishing a simple newsletter
- Learning to locate Internet addresses

Grade 3

Students entering Grade 3 have limited experience with using the left and right hand on the keyboard *so* we emphasize formal keyboarding in third grade. Because students are able to write sentences, they have begun to construct paragraphs that can be typed using the keyboard. These narratives and labeled poster drawings (e.g., the parts of a bee) with explanations and friendly letters are based on curricular study in Grade 2. At this point, students have already completed a simple newsletter and have a basic understanding of publishing. In addition, students have had an introduction to the Internet through visiting Web sites coordinated with curriculum. Experiences with SuperPrint, ClarisWorks, Netscape, and Classroom Publisher serve to assist students in the next level of skills at Grade 3.

In Grade 3, students continue to strengthen word processing, publishing, and presentation skills. As a part of this emphasis, they begin formal keyboarding to increase the speed of word processing. A portion of time both in the classroom and in the computer lab is spent practicing these hand skills. Students use All the Right Type, a keyboarding program, on a regular basis to increase the speed of word processing.

We have our students spend a great deal of time with the writing process. They write fables, beginning reports, and learn the basics of research using the electronic encyclopedia as well as the Internet to find information to support curricular study. Editing both in the classroom and on the computer is heavily emphasized. In using the computer, students learn to correct spelling errors and punctuation; use the formatting tools of bold, underline, centering, font changes and sizes; move text boxes; place graphics; alter graphics; and read for understanding. ClarisWorks, Netscape, Grolier's Encyclopedia, and HyperStudio are major software tools used by third graders.

Examples of curriculum projects completed in Grade 3 include introductory reports on the conservation of natural resources (Figure 5.21) and on Native Americans (Figure 5.22). Students learn to import images from the Internet through Netscape into their reports and also learn to wrap text around these imported graphics or drawings. Text wrapping refers to wrapping text around pictures or graphics in a report. A variety of reports are created, including outlines and written descriptions of information. Students learn to undertake beginning levels of research with the electronic encyclopedia and the Internet through careful modeling by third-grade teachers. At the end of the year, third graders write a fable with a moral, using the writing process (Figures 5.23 and 5.24). The fable is edited several times. Students prepare drawings to illustrate and sequence their fables. The drawings are then imported into HyperStudio where color is applied. Text is then added to each illustration. Students finish the project by recording their voice into HyperStudio and presenting their projects to their class.

By third grade, the layering of technology skills with language arts skills becomes quite apparent. Students are becoming competent in word processing and keyboarding. Editing skills are improving as students now are writing stories with four paragraphs. They are also completing history/social science and science reports. Students will end third grade with the following skills:

- Type with right and left hand

- Type at least 10 words per minute

- Import images from the Internet into reports

Figure 5.21.

Jonathan   Jan. 4, 1999

We should stop using lots of gasoline if it's short we could walk.
If you see some trash we could stop and pick it up.
We could recycle things like cans and bottles.
And if you go to a recycling center you make money.
The things humans do effect the planet.
We could try not to use natural resources.
And this is what could happen!

Figure 5.22.

Marc Conklin   3/29/99
Kwakiutl need natural resources to live. The Kwakiutl were Indains.
Kwakiutl needed cedar trees fro totem pole, conoes and other things.
Kwakiutl lived at tip of Alaska all the way to northern California. Thats
how Kwakiutl used their natural resouces.

Figure 5.23. The Sheep and the Wolf

The Sheep and the Wolf

By, Hayk Minasyan

One day a wolf was very hungry. He called to the sheep and he said, "Hi sheep! Is this you?"

"Oh hi wolf! How are you?"

"Hey sheep, come outside. They put me in this hot garden so we could play together," said the wolf.

"No thank you, wolf. I don't want to come outside. You come to my house."

"O.K." said the wolf, and he started to go to the sheep's house. When he went there he knocked on the door. the sheep wasn't opening the door. He knew that the wolf was going to eat him.

Then the wolf became angry. He broke the door and went inside. The sheep was hiding, but the wolf found him and said, Now you are mine!"

"Please don't hurt me wolf!" yelled the sheep.

"Why not? I am going to eat you up for my dinner because I am very hungry."

"O.k." said the sheep, "I am going to give you a nice dinner."

"No, you don't have a sheep," said the wolf. "Who cares? I am going to give you a better thing than sheep." said the sheep.

"O.K. but first let me see what it is." But the sheep had lied. He ran away from the wolf and the wolf couldn't find him any more.

THE END

The moral is: Talk to your enemy.

- Format graphic images
- Edit for spelling, punctuation, spacing, centering, indenting, capitalization, and grammatical correctness
- Find information in the electronic encyclopedia and on the Internet
- Outline research information
- Word process simple research reports and outlines

Figure 5.24. How Zebra Got His Stripes

How Zebra Got His Stripes

By Nicole McEntire

Many moons ago, there was a zebra. But unlike the zebras of today, he didn't have stripes. In fact all zebras were completely white. Zebra was a mean zebra. He would steal anything.

There was also a poor lion cub. She had one piece of gold left. The zebra didn't care. He just walked by and took it.

So, one day the rabbit, the bear, the duck and a lot more animals decided to have a meeting. They talked about what they should do about Zebra.

That night they put fake gold in a chest. When the animals heard Zebra opening the chest, they ran to the phone and called the police. They said "We have Zebra! We have Zebra!"

The police came over as fast as they could. They found Zebra and put him in jail.

A few months went by and the police let Zebra go. He met lots of friends.

Zebra learned that stealing is wrong. And from that day on, zebras have had stripes to remind them that stealing is wrong.

- Import illustrations into HyperStudio
- Storyboard text from a written fable
- Publish a story with illustrations using HyperStudio
- Present a simple multimedia story to an audience

Grade 4

Typically, our entering Grade 4 students will have initial keyboarding skills, type 5 to 10 words per minute, and will have had many beginning experiences with researching information using textbooks, the electronic encyclopedia, and the Internet. Incoming fourth graders have had an introductory experience in publishing a story using HyperStudio. Students will have had more experience with using tools in the software programs of ClarisWorks, HyperStudio, and Classroom Publisher. Editing skills associated with word processing are more advanced in that students readily know the rules for spacing, correcting errors in spelling and punctuation, as well as making basic changes in formatting text. Overall, students are ready to write extensive illustrated reports, assignments, and projects associated with the content of literature, history social/science, and science in Grade 4.

Technology skills emphasized in fourth grade include advanced features associated with software programs, such as:

- Cutting/pasting of text and graphics
- Use of text boxes
- Text wrap
- Altering graphics
- More sophisticated development of a newsletter

Fourth-grade students also learn new skills associated with ClarisWorks, including graphing data (bar, pie, and line graphing) and using spreadsheets for surveys.

Students learn specific research skills using the electronic encyclopedia and the Internet for information on projects and accessing different Web sites associated with curriculum studies, such as NASA for their study of space. Students will be involved in note taking to organize writing related to projects and reports. From developed notes and outlines, more extensive reports are created. These are then illustrated using images from the Internet, drawn illustrations, or art from software programs. In addition, our fourth graders participate in electronic mail (e-mail) through a pen-pal program with classrooms across the United States. Regular written exchanges are made throughout the year, typically November through May.

Fourth-grade students will also learn more about how to construct multimedia projects, including: (a) more advanced use of HyperStudio with the addition of voice, sound, and animation; (b) beginning use of a digital camera and camcorder to download photos into multimedia projects; and (c) introduction to the presentation software, PowerPoint.

During fourth grade, students continuously refine and expand the writing process associated with curriculum projects. Students are asked to complete extensive projects related to curricular concepts associated with schoolwide themes. Students write an autobiography and use the digital camera to import their picture; conduct surveys within the school on favorite pets, books, and so on; construct various types of graphs; and prepare reports on aspects of California history, using HyperStudio and PowerPoint (Figures 5.25 and 5.26). In addition, students create science reports from experiments completed in class.

During fourth grade, students are expected to use language arts skills for math, science, and history/social science curricula. Technology projects now require more thinking as projects become more integrated and

Figure 5.25. Survey Report

Daryn Watters   October 17, 1997

Survey Report

I surveyed 40 people. My question was "What's your favorite book?" Goosebumps received 20% Charlotte's Web received 5%. Dr. Seuss received 5%. Indian in the Cupboard received 1%. Bambie received 2% Other received 7%.

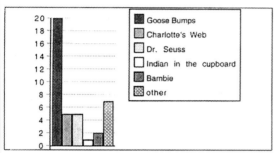

I used percentages. I used addition. I used multiplication, fractions, and decimals. I used these on my survey pie graph. My survey project and my survey bar graph.

The libraries need to know about my survey because I think they should know what kind of book's people like.

I Think I did a pretty good job. Next time, I would ask "What's your favorite animal?" I learned doing a survey is very hard.

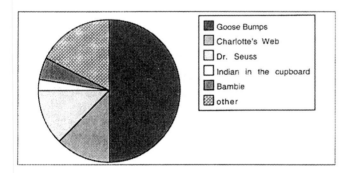

---

sophisticated. Students are expected to use research skills, develop notes and outlines, as well as present information. Overall, students will leave Grade 4 with the following technology skills:

- Keyboard 10 words per minute
- Insert images from the digital camera to written reports and news-letters
- Access different Web sites associated with curriculum research
- Text wrap around graphic images
- Edit regularly for spelling, punctuation, spacing, centering, indenting, capitalization, and grammatical correctness
- Animate and record voice and images in HyperStudio

Figure 5.26. Survey Report

Evan Filice   October 9, 1997

Survey Report

I surveyed 101 people—kids and adults. I asked "What is your favorite animal?" My results were: cheetah 16%, tiger 8%, lion 6%, cat 14%, wolf 13%, and other 44%.

I used fractions, decimals, division, multiplication, percentages and addition. I used addition to add up my totals. I used fractions and division to get my decimals. I rounded off to get my percentages.

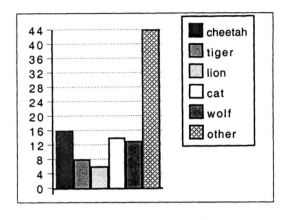

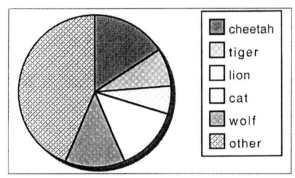

Zoos would want to know about my survey because they wouldn't want to show too many lions since lions received the lowest votes and not many people would want to come. They wouldn't get to much money because not that many people would want to come to the zoo.

I didn't do my hardest, I just wanted to see how good I did the first time. Next time, I will ask more people. I learned about percentages, fractions, addition, multiplication, and decimals.

- Take notes and outlines from the electronic encyclopedia and the Internet
- Word process a two-page research report
- Publish a newsletter using Classroom Publisher
- Prepare a basic report in HyperStudio and present it to an audience

Grade 5

Our entering fifth graders are expected to be able to word process and to have keyboarding skills to complete more demanding projects. Basic skills of research on the electronic encyclopedia and the Internet are also necessary for more advanced work. By now, our students have had significant experience with tools in ClarisWorks and HyperStudio. They are able to publish a newsletter using the tools in Classroom Publisher. Editing skills are also advanced in that students rewrite and re-edit regularly for spelling, punctuation, formatting, and grammatical correctness. Students have the ability to write illustrated reports and construct multimedia projects as preparation for advanced projects in Grade 5.

Students who have remained at Walt Disney School since their earlier grades are very competent in both technology skills and literacy skills. We have informally observed a third of Disney students occupying student leadership roles in technology, student newspaper, and yearbook staffs at the middle school. We have also observed that students who have not remained at Disney during all grades seem to learn technology skills quickly provided they have some English skills. It is difficult for second-language learners who arrive in our school during the intermediate grades to make the same kind of progress as students who have been at Disney since kindergarten.

Technology skills that will be emphasized in fifth grade include complete word processing skills and keyboarding skills so that students will be able to type a minimum of 20 words per minute. Publishing of projects and book and research reports occurs on a regular basis both in the computer lab and on computers in the regular classroom. Students regularly create HyperStudio stacks related to curriculum studies and add multimedia depending on the project. Students will learn advanced writing and publishing skills within PageMaker in the construction of the school newspaper, *The Disney Chronicle* (Figure 5.27). Students consistently use the digital camera and photo enhancement for pictures associated with articles in the newspaper. In addition, students begin to use Claris Homepage for producing their own Web site, learning the specific codes necessary for preparing a project for the Internet, as well as learning to upload their project to a Web server. Uploading is a process to place projects formally on the Internet.

Fifth graders also complete a variety of curriculum projects that are enhanced with sophisticated technology skills. For example, the students invest in the stock market (Figure 5.28) and chart and report their progress using the Internet and the graphing program in ClarisWorks. Other projects include:

- Creative writing for the project, "If I were in Charge of the World" (Figure 5.29), newspaper reporting, and editing for *The Disney Chronicle*

- Publishing the newspaper using PageMaker

- Research reports using the Internet and electronic encyclopedia on the Northern, Middle, and Southern colonies

- Biographical reports using HyperStudio

- Creating a Web site on the "western movement"

Figure 5.27. *The Disney Chronicle*

February is Black History Month

Martin Luther King Jr.

By

Jackie Rivera

In 1865, many black people from being slaves were free from slavery, but in some cases they were still treated the same way. Blacks who had to take the bus had to sit at the back of the bus, or stand while white people sat. As a boy this affected Martin Luther King Jr., a young bright black boy who had a dream that one day all people of every race would be treated equal.

Martin Luther King Jr. was born on January 15, 1929. His mom, Alberta, was a school teacher. His dad Martin Luther King Sr. was a Baptist Minister at the Ebenezer Baptist Church. Martin grew up and went to Morehouse College in Atlanta, Georgia but it was only for black men. Martin Luther King Jr. was an assistant pastor for his father at Ebenezer Baptist Church.

Martin Luther King married Coretta Scott. They had 4 children. Then all the black ministers gathered for a meeting and Martin was chosen as a minister at Dexter Baptist Church in Montgomery, Alabama. His whole family moved there in September 1954.

On April 3, 1968, he went to Memphis, Tennessee to support workers in the city. The next day, he was standing on the balcony in the room that he rented from the motel. He was talking to other people, and a bullet hit Dr. King and killed him.

The Disney Chronicle

First Edition   February 1999

Martin Luther King Jr. will be remembered no matter what happens because his spirit lives on.

Safe House Assembly

by Joshua Balderas

On January 15, 1999 a group of students from Burroughs High School and a fireman from the Burbank Fire Department came to Walt Disney. They came to teach us about the Safe House Program. They performed skits about when you should go to the safe house, or what choices you should make if you are in danger. One of the skits was about a man who lost his dog. He was pretending to look for his dog and he tried to grab a girl to come in his car.

Another topic they were talking about was what to do when you are feeling scared. If you think you're being followed, you should go to the Safe House and you will know that you will be safe inside. If you have other problems, like a broken leg or any other emergency, you should go into the Safe House for help.

Nicole McEntire

February 27, 1998

Figure 5.28. Stock Market Report

Stock Market Report

Hi, my name is Nicole. I bought stock in the Disney company. Each share was worth $69.75. My total investment was $976.50.

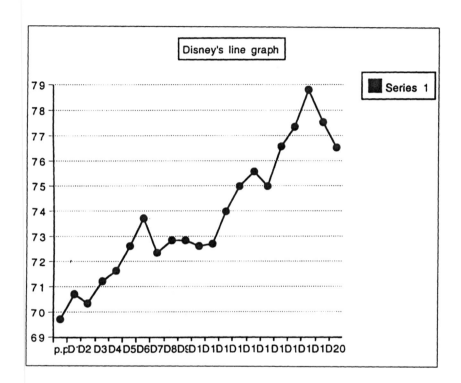

My stock's best day to sell was day 18. We would have made $126.84, if we sold our shares on that day.

My stock really didn't have a bad day, but the worst day would have been on day 2. We would have only made $8.82.

The kinds of math I used were: addition, subtraction, multiplication, the C Method, the backwards Z, and division.

I learned how to do a line graph, and how to manage information.

Each project demands that students be able to keyboard and word process with reasonable speed. By the time students reach fifth grade, technology is used as often as paper and pencil.

Students who leave the fifth grade at Walt Disney School have had years of experience using technology with curriculum. Technology has become an important tool for students in the creation of many kinds of complex projects. Students have also had many experiences with the skills of research, writing, editing, and presentation. Thus, by the end of fifth grade, students will leave for middle school with the following skills:

- Keyboard 20 words per minute
- Word process using a variety of software tools

Figure 5.29. If I Were in Charge of the World

- Design and format a document
- Edit for spelling, punctuation, and grammar
- Publish a newspaper using text boxes, formatting, graphics, text wrap, and photos
- Access information through the electronic encyclopedia or addresses on the Internet
- Animate and record voice, text, and images for a multimedia project
- Prepare and deliver a technology presentation to an audience
- Construct a Web site
- Upload projects to a Web server

Overall, this chapter has attempted to explain how technology skills integrate with a concept-based curriculum. Technology skills essentially work very closely with language arts process skills that students use to access the curriculum. By adding technology skills to the regular language arts skills, the thinking of students is elevated in that students are expected to apply these skills to curriculum projects. The traditional paper-and-pencil product can be transformed to a multimedia piece that involves not only writing in a one-dimensional format, but can integrate speaking, reading, and writing with technology tools that will create a multidimensional product. With technology added, students are required to think beyond the comprehension level. Using technology as a tool for curriculum will improve student literacy skills and thinking skills. One can simply verify this progress through observing demonstrated technology skills and the student products produced.

CHAPTER 6
Acquiring Tools: Hardware and Software

···

U nfortunately, most bad decisions about hardware and software purchases have little to do with a plan for how your students will use the technology. Hardware, or the physical equipment such as computers, monitors, printers, and so on, is often selected by school personnel "experts" or those in the school who have an interest in technology. Consequently, the hardware often turns out to benefit the special interests of a particular group of students in the school rather than all students in the school community. Software, on the other hand, refers to the programs that are loaded into the computer to perform specific functions, such as word processing (typing and formatting), publishing, networking, student tutorials for reading or math, games, and so on. A computer cannot work without software.

Most of the commercial market in student software is set up in a game or tutorial format to entice children. Typically parents, at the insistence of children, buy the latest program. This mentality must not rule in your school setting. Software must not be viewed as curriculum programs unto themselves or as separate from the regular core curriculum. Rather, software must be viewed as tools for children to use to create or enhance their work in curriculum study concepts or areas and must be linked to the student expectancies formulated in your early planning stages.

Most educational software is either tutorial or tool programs. A tutorial program is "closed-ended." Closed-ended software programs have an "end" to them. Once the child has figured out the pathways and played the various games inherent in them, there remains no more challenge. These programs are closed-ended. The software market continues to offer more and more games that entice parents and schools to buy them. "Open-ended" software, or tool programs, are programs that a child may use as he or she would paper and pencil. Children can continuously bring their curriculum projects to this software and produce a different result each time. These programs are open-ended and usually present a challenge to children. In addition, these programs always provoke thinking because children must use the program to produce a product rather than follow a pathway with its bells and whistles.

You don't want to make hardware and software decisions casually. These decisions should be made only after you have completed planning as to how students in the entire school community will use technology. The technology mission that has been formulated for students (see Chapters 2 and 3) will serve to protect you from making costly mistakes when buying hardware and software. This kind of thinking has prevented Walt Disney School from making costly errors over the past 10 years when funding was in short supply.

Because of the careful planning completed at Walt Disney School in 1988, wise hardware and software decisions were made (see Chapter 4). Our hardware purchases supported the establishment of a writing and publishing center for all students. All software purchased was open-ended for creative use, rather than tutorial use, by all grade levels. These decisions have strongly guided our efforts for the future. At the time of this writing, a second computer lab and file server are being established as well as an increased number of classroom computers connected to the local area network (LAN).

The Infrastructure:
The Importance of Networking

Before even considering hardware and software purchases, your school leadership team must look at the school's infrastructure or, to put it another way, the kind of wiring and conduit (tubing) that exists within the walls. The infrastructure is the most expensive item in establishing a technology program. An infrastructure is necessary to provide access to all classrooms through a local area network. A local area network is a network wiring plan from a central location within the school. The LAN carries wire from that centralized location through conduit to a lab and/or classrooms. With an established local area network, resources such as printers and file servers are shared. Instead of one student accessing a printer or a file through one computer, many students access the same printer or open files from a centralized file server. As long as the computer is on a network, files within the file server can be accessed regardless of the location of a workstation computer in the school.

Choices for Network Speed

A consideration for a LAN is the speed at which information will travel along the wires throughout the school. Every Macintosh comes with the capacity to link (computer to computer) through "Local Talk." However, in terms of speed of information going from one place to the next, it is like traveling in a covered wagon. With computers located long distances from a file server, the speed of accessing files becomes a significant issue. Ethernet is the speed most commonly used in local area networks (LANs). The speed of sending data over an Ethernet LAN compared to a Local Talk LAN resembles moving from covered-wagon speed to Model-T-Ford speed (10 packets per second). Fast Ethernet (100 packets per second) or Sonet, which uses fiber optic cable, transmits data signals 10 times faster than regular Ethernet. This might resemble moving from Model-T-Ford speed to racing-car speed at the Daytona 500.

Fiber optic cable allows for extremely fast transmission over long distances. Schools typically have several buildings that are far apart. With Ethernet, there is loss of speed over long distances. For the computer user this may mean more time is required to access files or to print a document. Consequently, you should consider installing fast Ethernet hubs placed at certain distances to minimize the loss of speed. A hub is a device that acts as a transmitter to maintain and push the data signal at a constant speed. Currently, wiring that is being completed in schools either in construction or being remodeled is fiber optic cable and fast Ethernet.

Linked into the LAN are workstations and a local file server. A file server is a computer that acts as a file cabinet for storing all student files. This computer keeps all student files by name and can be accessed from any computer that is connected to the network. A Macintosh file server runs the program AppleTalk to administer files, and a software program, Mac Manager, to manage student files. These programs eliminate the management nightmare of using floppy disks for storing student work.

Investigate the Wiring

In order to establish a LAN, your school leadership team must determine what wiring currently exists in the school as well as any other wiring necessary to allow access by students. To plan for appropriate hardware and software with the infrastructure in mind, your team should diligently answer a series of questions. The following network planning questions must be answered to allocate funds:

- What wiring currently exists? Diagram this on an actual school plan. What category is the data cable wiring? Data wiring can range in size and number of wires contained in a cable (e.g., Category 3 with three pairs of wires, or the recommended Category 5 with five pairs of wires).

- What central location is favorable for wiring to be centralized?

- Where can a LAN first be located (as in a computer lab)?

- How will student files be managed? Through a file server in a lab setting?

- What kind of speed do you want on your network? Do you want Ethernet, Fast Ethernet, or fiber optic connections in the computer lab or classrooms?
- What network software will be used to manage student files? AppleShare? Mac Manager?
- What type of conduit exists between classrooms and the electrical room? Does this conduit contain electrical or data wiring? What cost is involved in establishing connections between classrooms, library, or office?
- What kind of access will be planned for Internet services? Modem access to a provider? Which provider? Integrated Service Digital Network (ISDN) line or ISDN provider? DSL (Digital Service Line)?

Based on the answers to these network planning questions, your team is ready to plan both long-term and short-term goals as to how to begin your technology program and certainly where to allocate costs for setting up a LAN.

Making Decisions on Hardware

Hardware decisions can best be made when you have determined a network plan as well as a plan of how technology will be used by students. School leadership teams often do not have a basic understanding of the networking side of technology needed to make wise hardware decisions, especially in the sharing of resources. For example, a neighboring school consulted with our leadership team to plan for hardware purchases. Because its team did not understand the power of networking, the school purchased dot matrix printers for each classroom rather than two high-quality laser printers that could have been shared among several classrooms, creating great access and yet saving money.

Creating the greatest access to technology tools has always been the guiding principle of our hardware purchases; that is, we want the same kind of access to technology tools as for the traditional tools of paper and pencil. Also, providing students time for using the technology tools is always a challenge. At Disney, we strive to give students more and more time with these tools. Thus our hardware decisions to acquire more and more student workstations are always based on this goal.

Because of an increasing enrollment at Disney, we knew that our one computer lab was not providing enough time for teachers and students to use technology tools. In fact, our increased enrollment was cutting down on the time we originally had scheduled for students. So, for the past 3 years our priority has been to purchase workstations to increase steadily the number of computers in classrooms to extend technology access. However, we realized that the time in the computer lab with the entire class delivered the greatest amount of access for students. Our short-term goal is to create another computer lab in the next year; our long-term goal is to make each classroom a computer lab. In new construction that is being planned at Walt Disney School, each of the 10 new classrooms will have the capacity to be a computer lab.

Minimum Requirements for a Workstation

Since acquiring workstations should be a high hardware priority, your team should be aware of minimum requirements. Hardware dealers are notorious for selling cheap and useless workstations that soon will be out of date or will require additional parts. What may sound like a good buy may be soon out of date or involve added expense. It is a good idea to research what workstations to purchase. In considering workstations, the computer chip (e.g., Pentium III), sufficient memory, hard drive space, processor speed, operating system, Ethernet capability, modem, installed CD-ROM/DVD, and kind of monitor must be considered. Figure 6.1 displays minimum requirements for both IBM and Macintosh workstations.

Warranties and repair considerations must be carefully researched. With more than 500 students accessing our computers each week, constant repairs are needed. When a workstation is down, certain students do not have access to that computer to do work. In order to cope with the demands of repairs, purchasing workstations from reliable companies is a necessity. For example, the Dell Computer Company guarantees its computers for 3 years. If anything goes wrong with the computer, they will send a replacement computer at their cost while the school's computer is being repaired. With these considerations in mind, you are ready to begin the process of selecting hardware (Figure 6.2).

Making Hardware Decisions

Hardware Step 1

The initial step is to inventory the technology tools that are in the school now.

- What computer workstations currently exist?
- How old is the current equipment?
- Can the current equipment be used in a network?

If your school has older computers, such as Apple IIes or IBM 386s, you must weigh the cost of outfitting these computers against purchasing newer equipment that requires no additional expense. With technology

Figure 6.1. Minimum PC Requirements for Workstations

Minimum PC Requirements for Workstations

Macintosh Personal Computer	IBM-Compatible Personal Computer
Operating System 8.5.1 or better	Windows NT or Windows 98
Minimum 300 MHz G3 Processor	Minimum Pentium II 300 MHz Processor
Minimum 64 RAM	Minimum 64 RAM
Minimum 6 Gig Hard Drive	Minimum 6 Gig Hard Drive
Fast Ethernet Capable	Fast Ethernet Capable
Monitor-Millions of colors	Monitor-Millions of colors
56 Kbs modem	56 Kbs modem

changing at such a fast rate, operating systems, memory requirements, and hard drive space are critical to operating the newer software. Older computer workstations in schools do not have the capacity to handle the demands of this new software.

Hardware Step 2

The second step in selecting hardware is to revisit the student expectancies and activities dictated in the technology plan. Overall, these expectancies must guide your hardware selection. How we expect our students to use technology and their access to these tools is the reason hardware is purchased. Remember that our chief goal started with improving student writing and evolved to using technology as a research and communication tool.

Hardware Step 3

Next determine what hardware tools will assist in realizing your student expectancies. We first purchased eight Macintosh SE 20 computers, with one of these workstations as a dedicated file server linked with six existing Apple IIe computers; a laser printer; and a scanner to set up a writing and publishing lab. These hardware tools related directly to our student writing expectancy. Our first overall plan (see Chapter 4) illustrates the relationship of purchasing hardware to improving student writing. The tools we chose in 1999 reflect the improvements in technology as

Figure 6.2. Acquiring Hardware for Student Use

Acquiring Hardware for Student Use

1. Inventory what you have. How can these be used for the greatest number of students?

2. What are the student expectancies and activities dictated in the technology plan?

3. What hardware tools will assist you in realizing student expectancies?

4. What support (construction and financial) is currently available from your district or community?

5. Secure and plan present financial resources from budgets and fund-raising.

6. Invest appropriately based on plan priority. List your priorities.

---

related to our expectation that students will use technology tools in all areas of the curriculum. We also intend that students learn to find and manage information, communicate, and produce meaningful products. As a result, our choices for hardware for 1999 include:

- Eight Macintosh G3 workstations
- Two HP DeskJet Ethernet color printers
- Two Netgear 16 Port 10 Base-T Hubs for the computer lab
- Four Asante 10 Base-T Hubs for classrooms
- One G3 333 megahertz file server
- Fifteen 128 MB memory for lab workstations

Hardware Step 4

Investigating the support currently available from your district or community is the fourth step in making decisions on hardware. Because technology hardware changes so rapidly, it is necessary to access expertise outside of the school for hardware recommendations. Districts are now employing personnel to direct or coordinate technology. Depending on the knowledge of district personnel, a school can gain the first level of support here, especially in matters of network wiring, electrical support, and hardware recommendations. In addition, Districts are receiving funding through State Departments of Education for distribution to schools.

However, the community is the second most important resource. Many businesses outside the school are anxious to support technology growth in education. When we first began, Lockheed provided advice and assistance. Apple representatives and local repair businesses continue to assist us with hardware, networking, repairs, and training.

Hardware Step 5

Securing financial resources is the fifth step in the process of making decisions on hardware. Often schools ask how our school was able to secure funding. There literally was no funding for our technology program when we started. The important factor is that we continued to plan what we would do as if we already had the money. Even to this day, we continue to plan in that manner. We have never worried about getting the funding. When a school has a plan, the funding will come.

Begin by allocating existing site funding from budgets and fund-raisers based on your technology plan and plan for future funding. Show your technology plan, with its explicit student expectancies, to your community partners. When your plans are clear, the business community will probably support your efforts.

Hardware Step 6

The final and most important step is to invest appropriately, based on the priorities set forth in your technology plan. Depending on the level of funding, develop a priority list of tasks you want to complete. For most schools the priorities include establishing network connections, acquiring hardware and software, and long-term investing in infrastructure for continued expansion and growth.

By completing these six steps in the hardware survey in Figure 6.2, you will go a long way toward eliminating guesswork and will develop wise plans for hardware selection. It is important to realize that this planning survey will need to be repeated on a yearly basis as the technology program develops over the years.

Making Software Decisions

When considering software, you must think about three different software categories: network, curricular, and utility.

Network Software

Network software is primarily for managing the local area network (LAN) and distributing student files. For example, AppleShare and Mac Manager are two Apple Computer products that are recommended for Apple file servers. This software allows networked workstation computers anywhere in the school to share resources such as printers, as well as to open individual files in the file server. This type of software is necessary for a school LAN. Additionally, because each student, teacher, and staff member has a file in the file server, there is no need for large numbers of floppy disks to store information for all individuals in the school. Each school planning a LAN should consider the purchase of this type of software for overall school management.

Curricular Software

The second type of software is curricular. Most educators are familiar with this kind of software. Curricular software can be closed-ended or open-ended. To review, closed-ended software, such as tutorial programs or games, has specific preset pathways the students will follow. The problem with this software is that students soon learn all the pathways to the result and then are bored with the program. These software programs become "edu-tainment" for children instead of provoking creative thinking. Further, these programs are not tools that children can use creatively with curriculum.

On the other hand, open-ended programs, such as those for word processing, publishing, graphics enhancements, slide shows, Internet browsing, electronic encyclopedias, and so on, are tools children can and should use with the curriculum. These programs are not edu-tainment but tools that will build a set of specific technology skills integrated with the language arts skills embedded in curriculum. As a result, student thinking and creativity are elevated beyond simply the comprehension levels of thinking to application, analysis, synthesis, and evaluation levels in the completion of projects directly related to the curriculum.

Utility Software

The third type of software is utility software. A common utility software is *blocking* software for Internet use. This type of utility program blocks out Web sites inappropriate for students through a subscriber service. Updates are sent to a school LAN on a weekly or monthly basis through ISDN Internet addresses or through a modem.

A virus protection program is another type of utility software. With any Internet use or disk use, virus protection software prevents computer hard drives from becoming infected by a computer virus that could delete files or "crash" a computer. A virus can delete files or prevent them from being accessed. This is termed a *crash*. Virus protection programs are very important to protect the data, particularly in the file server of a school. The program scans and screens any files coming into the workstations. A third kind of utility software program is one that fixes software crashes, hard disk problems, lost files, or system software problems. Such a utility

Figure 6.3. Acquiring Software for Student Use

Acquiring Software for Student Use

1. Inventory what software you have. How is this software currently being used?

2. What are the student expectancies and activities dictated in the technology plan?

3. What software tools will assist you in realizing student expectancies?

4. Secure financial resources by identifying funding from budgets, fund-raisers, grants, and so forth.

5. Invest appropriately based on plan priority. Consider type of hardware and memory requirements the software recommends. Purchase software according to priority.

---

program is a must for ongoing maintenance of all computers in the school (Figure 6.3).

Software Step 1

With an understanding of these three types of software, your school staff can participate in selecting appropriate software for the school. The first place to start is to inventory the software that currently exists in the school. This is much the same as the first step in selecting hardware. With software, however, check to see what version of software exists and whether it is outdated. Newer computers cannot use "old software" efficiently. Check the system requirements on the software box. Locate any software licenses that may exist. Once a license has been granted, software can be updated at a minimal cost.

Software Step 2

The second step is to review again the student expectancies and activities dictated in the technology plan. Software selections must reflect how you want students to use technology. Determine what programs are closed-ended versus open-ended and how potential programs will support these student expectancies. For each expectancy, list a type of software program that is needed.

Software Step 3

Once a list of the types of software programs has been determined, the next step is to be specific as to which programs you want to select. One of your first basic decisions should be what word processing and publishing program will be used. Several programs exist, including Microsoft Office 97 and 98, ClarisWorks, Microsoft Works, and others. Be aware that some programs, such as Office 97 or 98, include a variety of programs in one package, such as word processing, publishing, spreadsheet, database, Web publishing, and presentation software. Back in 1989, we selected Microsoft Works because it contained four programs, including word processing, database, spreadsheet, and communication tools. It was also cost-effective for our limited budget. Later on, because the memory requirements of the Microsoft Works software increased beyond our computer memory capacity, we opted for ClarisWorks (now AppleWorks) because the memory requirements are not as extensive.

In addition, be aware of the level of difficulty of some of these programs for students. When making a major purchase of software, always preview the software with staff members before the money is spent to determine if it is easy to teach and to use with students. Most software companies will allow schools to preview the programs to determine usability with students. One of the main problems we had was choosing software that we could use with limited-English students. The programs that were selected had to be *user friendly* for these students.

Software Step 4

Identifying your funding from budgets, fund-raisers, grants, and so on, is the fourth step in software selection. A portion of your budget should always be allocated to software. The budget must not all be used for hardware. Software is constantly being updated and changed. Each school year, money will need to be set aside for these updates and changes. District volume purchases of software can assist you in saving money when purchasing software.

Along with software updates, there will be memory upgrades for computers. Your team must be ever aware of the memory requirements of software. Even though the addition of memory is a hardware issue, it goes hand in hand with software upgrades. These are the hidden costs in your technology plan (see discussion of Disney Technology Plan budget in Chapter 4).

Software Step 5

The last step is to invest appropriately, based on the priority established by the student expectancies in your technology plan. Rank order the software that you need to purchase as well as what software you would like to purchase over a 3-year period. Select software for the greatest student access. Site licenses are expensive, so the software you buy must service the greatest number of students. Site licenses can cost as much as $3,000. Some software companies will provide a licensing cost per workstation. For example, ClarisWorks 5.0 costs $24 per workstation. Multiplied by the number of computers, our software cost is approximately $1,500. When special interest software is purchased for one group of students, access is denied to other students in the school. This is not cost-effective and does not allow maximum student access.

By completing the software survey in Figure 6.3, you will continue the pattern of wise decisions for using funds. As with the network and hardware surveys, this survey will need to be completed yearly to plan effectively for needed software. These software selections will always link to the kind of hardware purchased as well as to the networking plans. Overall, yearly planning will continue to further the development and expansion of your school's technology program for many years.

CHAPTER 7

Using the Internet to Enhance Curriculum and Instruction

···

The Internet is an exciting new resource we can use to improve learning. Within seconds, students can visit museums, libraries, businesses, news organizations, the White House, NASA, the U.S. Weather Service, and other agencies all over the world to learn first-hand information quicker and more up to date than any encyclopedia. Students, in turn, can respond by uploading curriculum projects onto the Internet or sending e-mail to these organizations, receiving direct responses on the concepts being studied.

With using the Internet as a tool, students learn to take charge of their learning by participating in real-world learning projects. School science projects involving "real" data take on new meaning as students work with the scientists at National Geographic Kidsnet. The Internet also enables students to grasp difficult concepts through visual multimedia formats presented on most Web sites, such as http://www.weather.com. Thus, the Internet can help students attack more challenging content material through the completion of curricular projects. For example, for their stock market reports, Disney fifth-grade students access the Internet every day to monitor their own selected stock. The research and daily updated information on the stock market form a part of their final research report.

You will find that the Internet generally motivates and assists those students who may not be successful otherwise. The interactive nature of the Internet entices and creates tremendous interest in learning. Limited-English students really benefit from the Internet's multimedia approach to presenting information. Where textbooks tend to be extremely challenging for these students, the Internet's visual displays assist them in grasping curricular concepts. The added dimension of responding through e-mail to a live audience on the Internet also creates relevance for students by linking them to the real world.

Using the Internet as a tool with curriculum and instruction begins with the networking plan at your school. Networking (see "The Infrastructure: The Importance of Networking" in Chapter 6) is a sharing of resources via your school wiring; students are linked to the Internet through a simple phone line, an installed Integrated Service Digital Network (ISDN), or DSL (Digital Service Line) connected to a network plan or local area network (LAN). When a LAN is in place in the school, students will be able to access the Internet from any location in the school.

What Is the Internet?

The Internet is a general term for a large group of computers all over the world linked to one another so that users and computers themselves can exchange information. To exchange information, protocols such as Hypertext Transport Protocol (HTTP) are used. A *protocol* is a format or code that must be applied to information for the Internet so that information can be exchanged. HTTP is the protocol that currently transfers Internet or World Wide Web information because it can integrate text, virtual images, and sound. Older protocols such as FTP, Gopher, Mosaic, and TELNET still exist but are not used as often because they cannot format information using images, video, or sound.

The World Wide Web (www, the Web, or W3) is a hypermedia information system. *Hypermedia* refers to the capacity to present virtual, on-screen pages—combining text, graphics, audio, and video—that link to other pages. "The Web" technically refers to the whole gamut of hypermedia/hypertext servers that present virtual, on-screen pages combining text, graphics, audio, and video.

What Is Hypertext?

The Web allows a user to access information in a nonlinear way through *hypertext links*. The idea behind hypertext is that instead of reading text in a rigidly linear structure (such as from page to page in a book), a user can jump from link to link, page to page, across sites and servers. For example, Yahoo, a popular search engine, can help to locate an area of interest such as "American museums." Search engines are Internet indexes that can locate Web sites topically or by name. Yahoo will list American museums such as the National Gallery of Art or the Getty Museum. By clicking on the museum name, which is a hypertext link, one can immediately go to that museum's Web site. The Getty *home page*, which is the first page at the site, is an index to other pages within the museum site. The hypertext links on the Getty home page may take the user to other museums in a matter of seconds. Thus the user can access art information from all across the world.

The Web is also *cross-platform*, which means that a user can access Web information easily from both Macintosh and IBM compatible computers running different operating systems, for example Windows 95/98 or Macintosh OS. Access to the Web can be achieved simply by a modem connected to a computer making a phone call through a phone line. A user can simply use a modem, a hardware device within or attached to the computer used, to call an Internet provider such as America Online (AOL) to access the Web. An Internet provider is an intermediary between the user and the Internet. More sophisticated connections involve a direct Internet connection through an installed ISDN (Integrated Service Digital Network), DSL (Digital Service Line), or T1 (a high-speed Net access phone line). A T1 line is capable of handling large numbers of users, as in a local college, whereas an ISDN line can handle users within a small school or department.

What Is an Internet Browser?

Access to the Web is gained through a software application called a browser. A Web browser enables you to access the Web and get information from a server (a computer that stores information). With a browser, you can view and select hypertext links on Web pages. The links are always highlighted so that you can easily see them. The browser's job is to speak to the contacted server (e.g., The National Gallery of Art) using the HTTP protocol and to retrieve the documents from that server. The browser will then interpret the HTML code contained in the document, format it, and display it. The first page that appears is called the home page. From the home page, you can access the other information within that site through hypertext links. The most common browsers are Netscape Navigator and Microsoft's Internet Explorer.

Web Search Engines

The Web is a system of information distributed globally across thousands of Web sites, each of which contributes the space for the information it publishes. Search engines such as Yahoo, Yahooligans, Alta Vista, and Web Crawler, to name some, help to provide a means of sorting through information, much the same as an encyclopedia does (Figure 7.1). Many of these search engines also have a *search box* that helps students with locating topics, authors, or titles. Yahoo lists general categories of information alphabetically. A benefit of researching on the Internet is that the Web allows a user to view information at a specific Web site without having to save that information on the user's hard disk (the internal disk memory). Thus, students can access many Web sites while looking for specific information.

Figure 7.1.

Uniform Resource Locators (URLs)

Each Web site and each page or bit of information on that site has a unique address. This address is called a Uniform Resource Locator (URL). The URL for the Getty Museum is *http://artsednet.getty.edu*. The first part of the URL (http) tells the browser it's looking for a Web page. The remainder of the address gives the name of the Web server (computer) that holds the page (artsednet.getty.edu).

The Web is also dynamic because a majority of sites are updated continuously by Web publishers. For example, news organizations such as CNN or Nando Times are updated continuously, 24 hours a day. Other sites are also constantly being added to. According to Daggett (1998), the information on the Internet doubles every 6 months. Also, libraries, educational institutions, government, businesses, and others, provide a user with more current information than can be found in newspapers, television, or books. There is no question that the Web is a valuable research tool for students. (For a listing of URLs and definitions of other Internet terms, see the Internet Glossary in Resource B.)

Developing a Basic Internet Connection

Contrary to most thinking, establishing an Internet connection is easy. For a basic set-up within a school library, three items are necessary:

- An adequate computer with a modem
- An installed phone line
- An Internet provider

Step 1: Obtain an Adequate Computer

An adequate computer is a power computer with at least:

- 64 Mg RAM
- Six gigabytes HD (Hard Drive)
- 300 Pentium III or G3 megahertz processor
- Windows NT, Windows 98, or Mac 8.5.1 system software
- 56 Kbps (kilobits per second) modem internally installed or external
- browser software (e.g., Netscape) (see Figure 6.1)

To clarify: Memory is identified as either RAM or ROM. Random-access memory (RAM) allows computer software programs to open and perform functions. ROM or hard drive memory, identified in bytes, allows space for system software (e.g., Windows 95), program applications (e.g., Microsoft Word), and personal files to be stored. HD space can be converted to random-access memory if needed. These specifications are standard features on today's Macintosh or IBM/ IBM-compatible power computer.

Step 2: Establish a Phone Connection

An installed phone line is the second step in establishing a connection. The computer will be connected to this phone line through the modem. The computer modem is a device that can link the library computer to another outside computer through a phone line. With an internal modem, there will be a phone jack (as with your telephone at home) on the side or in the back of the computer. An external modem looks like a small box with a phone jack; the external connects to the back of the computer.

Step 3: Establish an Internet Provider

The last step is to establish an Internet provider. The most common Internet provider is America Online (AOL). Internet providers usually charge a monthly fee for services (e.g., $20). However, with schools, there are many other ways to establish a provider. For example, the Los Angeles County Office of Education offers School Districts in Los Angeles County a 56 Kbps (kilobits per second) line free of charge. Still, a direct Internet provider can be obtained through the phone companies or other providers for monthly fees.

To access an Internet provider, the modem on the library computer dials the phone number, for example, of America Online. The Web server at America Online answers the phone, asks for a password, and then immediately provides the library computer the America Online home page. From the home page, your students can explore the Internet through various hypertext links.

Establishing an Advanced Internet Connection

Establishing an advanced Internet connection in which all computers within the school are connected to the Internet is also not difficult. Again, three conditions must be met:

- Establish a local area network (LAN)
- Purchase an Internet Router
- Install either an ISDN (Integrated Service Digital Network), DSL, or a T1, a large, high-speed line that can accommodate many users

Step 1: Establish a Local Area Network

The first criterion in establishing Internet access is that your school must have a local area network (LAN; see Chapter 6). The LAN can be as simple as a computer lab within the school where all computers are linked to a central file server, or as complex as linking a computer lab to other outside computers through the file server. The whole plan depends on the wiring in the school. A school must have the wiring to carry the data signals from location to location throughout the school from a centralized location. Without the wiring in place in all school buildings, the ISDN, DSL, or T1 phone line carrying the Internet will not be able to be accessed from locations in the school.

Remember that the computers in the LAN that access the Internet must adhere to the requirements for a simple Internet connection. Even in a school LAN, however, your leadership team can determine which computers will access the Internet. Connecting all school computers to the

Internet on the LAN is technically possible. However, Internet computers should have at least 64 MEG, current operating systems such as Windows 95/98 for IBM or system 7.6.1 or above for Macintosh, and processor speeds of 300 megahertz or higher. Current versions of Netscape and Microsoft browsers also demand these minimum computer requirements. Otherwise, accessing the Internet will be a very slow and tedious process.

Step 2: Obtain an Internet Router

The purchase of an Internet router is the second requirement for schoolwide access to the Internet. There are many types of routers with specific specifications at a variety of prices ($2,000 and higher). An Internet router is a hardware device that acts as a gateway between two or more networks. Routers, which are actually types of computers, are designed to comprehend the various protocols the respective networks use. A LAN usually runs on Ethernet, while the Internet runs on the standard protocol, TCP/IP. A router is designed to translate and route information back and forth from Ethernet to TCP/IP in the LAN.

TCP/IP is the basic language by which all Internet computers talk to each other and send the tiny chunks of information that make up a Web page. For an Internet provider like AOL (America Online) there is no need to worry about TCP/IP, but for a school LAN, TCP/IP must be configured with a specific numerical address within the router itself as well as in all the workstations. These settings are found in the control panels of a computer's system software. Each computer in the LAN accessing the Internet has within its system software (e.g., Windows 98 or Macintosh 8.1) TCP/IP. TCP/IP has various settings, depending on the type of Internet connection to be established.

Step 3: Get an Internet Provider

Acquiring an Internet provider is the third step for an advanced Internet connection. Internet service, when it was first offered to schools by AT&T, MCI, and GTE in 1996-1997, was free of charge. These companies were willing to install ISDN (Integrated Service Digital Network) lines free. ISDN is the digital telephone system that has been touted as the replacement for the slow and noisy analog phone lines. It carries voice, data, and graphic images up to 128 Kbps (kilobits per second). Current DSL (Digital Service Line) is 10 times faster than an ordinary ISDN for about $50 per month.

With the proposed funding by the federal government (E-Rate), school districts will have assistance in acquiring the hardware and wiring necessary for establishing Internet connections at a reduced rate. Districts will be able to install T1 lines (phone lines that are leased by big companies, schools, and the government for high-speed 1,544 Kbps Internet access with video conferencing capabilities) and the hardware necessary to establish connections across the district. T1 lines can accommodate many users and carry data and images more effectively. A T1 line will also give school districts the capacity for video conferencing. Schools should plan for T1 lines if possible. The number of students and staff using the Internet will always be increasing. ISDN lines with 128 Kbps will become crowded as number of users increases. When there are too many students or staff on an ISDN line, logging onto the Internet becomes very slow and access may be denied entirely if there are too many users.

Keys to Using the Internet With Curriculum

The first key to understanding the use of the Internet with curriculum is to recognize that the Internet is both a research and a response tool for your students. As a research tool, the Internet is more current than any printed media. Students have the benefit of accessing the most current information beyond what is contained in their textbooks or encyclopedias. However, with the large volumes of information out on the Internet, students will need to be taught the skills to access that information.

The Internet is also a response tool for communication, through e-mail to a Web site to ask questions of the scientists at NASA or to a congressperson to ask about an issue the class is studying. In addition, students can post information to a school or district Web site to share on the Internet. Students using the Internet can research not only information on Web sites, but can also post curriculum projects they have created. For examples of student projects, please refer to the student gallery at the Disney Web site, *http://www.burbank.k12.ca.us/schools/main_wdc.html*.

Using student expectancies to define what you want your students to do with the Internet is the second key. Let me stress that your team must have a clear picture of how the Internet will be used by your students as a research and response tool to further the curriculum concepts and learning. For example, an expectancy we have for all Disney students is to learn basic research skills by using the Internet for curriculum projects.

Begin With Basic Internet Skills

To start the research process, students must first be taught the basic skills to use the Internet with the curriculum. These technology skills of Internet research build on other language arts research skills.

- The first skill to teach students is to locate a Web site or URL (Uniform Resource Locator)
- Second, students will need to learn how to navigate within that Web site address

- The last of these skills to teach students is how to work with a search engine such as Yahoo

Yahoo and other search engines operate the same as an encyclopedia with many layers of hypertext links. It is important that teachers model these Internet skills to build understanding of the way the Web is constructed and how to navigate it. Be prepared for your students to need much practice with these first skills.

Organizing Research Information From the Internet

Next is teaching the skills of downloading text and pictures. Students will need to sort through the information and use copy-and-paste techniques to create a page with notes for topics under study. Within the browser (e.g., Netscape) there are copy-and-paste functions under the Edit menu. What is copied from the Internet can be pasted into a page of notes in a word processing program such as Microsoft Word. Pages from the Internet can also be printed. Students will need to be able to organize the information taken from the Internet into notes. These notes then form the basis of written projects. Additionally, pictures can be added to notes by using screen captures, or holding down the mouse button to copy the picture onto the hard drive.

Using E-Mail

After your students have mastered downloading text and pictures and are fairly accomplished at note taking, lead them to e-mail. A good way to begin implementing e-mail is first to respond as a class to a local congressperson or an organization such as NASA. Students can send e-mail using the class address to get information, ask questions, or express opinions to various organizations. Writing skills, specifically letter writing, are applied to real-world situations that are meaningful to students, especially when their e-mail is answered. At Disney, each class has an e-mail address.

Creating Student Web Pages

Now it's time to teach students how to create Web pages. These skills are more appropriate for fourth or fifth graders as applied to their curriculum projects. Displaying projects on the Web provides practice in extending skills from the storyboarding skills built in third grade when interactive books of fables are developed (see Figures 5.4 and 5.8 in Chapter 5).

Disney students have participated in creating the Disney School Web Site (Figure 7.2). Students learned HTML (Hypertext Markup Language) to prepare Web pages in order to prepare curriculum projects for uploading

Figure 7.2.

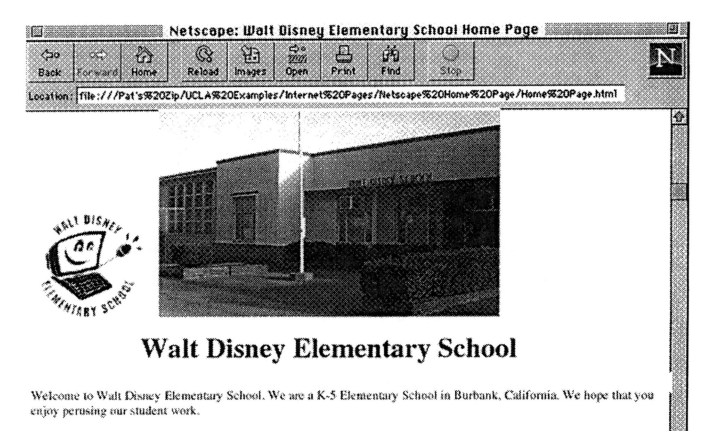

onto the Internet through the District's Web server (Figure 7.3). Tech team students this year are working on preparing a history/social science report on the Western movement for posting on the Internet. After writing their report, they will format it in HTML and learn to upload the project onto the Internet.

Coordinate Internet Use With Curriculum Concepts

The third key is to coordinate Internet use with curriculum concepts through concept-based planning (see Chapter 3). Because the information on the Internet is vast and requires a great amount of time to sort through, focusing the curriculum around concepts will help to narrow the volume of information searched. When the curriculum is not focused, the Internet may become edu-tainment rather than a companion tool for curriculum. Also, *free falling*, or allowing students to explore the Internet unsupervised, can compromise access security and open the door to inappropriate sites, even with blocking software. This can occur because of the layers of hypertext links across many Web sites. Not all Internet blocking software can screen out the layers of links that may be inappropriate.

Figure 7.3. Hypertext Markup Language

```
<HTML>
<HEAD>
<TITLE>Walt Disney Elementary School Home Page</TITLE>
</HEAD>
<BODY BGCOLOR= "<35>6495ED">
<HR WIDTH=100%>
<IMG SRC = "Disney Logo 2.GIF">
<IMG SRC= "web kids.jpg">
<H1 ALIGN=CENTER>Walt Disney Elementary School</H1>
<HR WIDTH=100%>
<P>Welcome to Walt Disney Elementary School. We are a K-5 Elementary School in Burbank,
California. We hope that you enjoy perusing our student work.</P>
<H2><A HREF= "Interactive Books/Interactive Books.html">Student Surveys</A></H2>
<P>The following are surveys taken by students in Mr. Carman's fourth grade class</P>
<H2><A HREF= "Stock Market Reports/Stock Market Reports.html">Stock Market
Reports</A></H2>
<P>Students in Mr. Carman's and Mrs. DeAngelis' classes have tracked the progress of several
different companies e.g., Apple Computer, IBM, Disney, Sony, Nordstroms and many more.</P>
<H2><A HREF= "Disney Gazette/Disney Gazette.html">The Disney Gazette</A></H2>
<P>Our student newspaper</P>
<H2><A HREF= "Tech Plan/Tech Plan.html">The Disney Technology Plan</A></H2>
<P>Our acclaimed technology plan.</P>
<H2><A HREF= "Tour of Disney/Tour.html">Tour of Disney Elementary</A></H2>
<H2><A HREF= "Evelia's Netscapade Folder/Evelia's Netscapade.html">Evelia's
Netscapade</A></H2>
</BODY>
</HTML>
```

Plan for Bandwidth

Becoming aware of bandwidth is the fourth key to using the Internet with the curriculum. *Bandwidth* refers to the number of signals that an ISDN line or T1 line can accommodate. The greater the number of students accessing the Internet, the greater the need for bandwidth. When there are too many students accessing the Internet on an ISDN line, the large number of signals jams, reducing speed of access or preventing access. An ISDN line can easily accommodate one or two classrooms of students. However, where hundreds of students are accessing the Internet, as in a university, a DSL line, T1 line, or several T1 lines are needed. Therefore, schools sometimes may need to add one or more ISDN, DSL, or T1 lines to accommodate access to the Internet.

In summary, the Internet is a real-world tool for students to use with the curriculum for both research and response. Not only can the Internet motivate students, it can also help them to take charge of their learning. However, the use of the Internet is dependent upon the network plan within the school. A network connection can be simple, with one computer, or more complex, with many computers. Both plans require accessing the Web through ISDN or regular phone lines. Once connections have been established, student expectancies and a concept-based curriculum must guide the use of the Internet with students. This focus will build the necessary student research and response skills for future work in a global society.

CHAPTER 8
Training School Staff Through Collaborative Models

The importance of training all staff to use technology cannot be overemphasized. Weaving technology into curriculum depends primarily on the training of the classroom teacher and the support staff surrounding the teacher. As teachers are empowered to use technology tools themselves, so they will empower their students. Only teachers can bring the creativity of technology to the curriculum and thereby enhance student learning.

There are several reasons why all staff should be trained to use technology, but the primary reason is to empower each person to fulfill the technology mission formulated in your school plan. Staff training is the best way to build a shared commitment to the technology mission statement and student expectancies at all grade levels. Training is a tool to build a "collective consciousness" among staff who are hesitant to use technology. When few staff are trained, the capacity for building this collective consciousness is seriously diminished, and the importance of implementing technology is relegated to only those who are interested.

Creating an atmosphere of collegial support is the second reason for training all staff. Learning how to use technology demands great change. Cultivating an atmosphere of support helps to reduce anxiety and to encourage risk taking by staff. Additionally, training fosters professional interactions and a shared language among teachers about using technology. This shared technology language allows these new skills to be incorporated into each teacher's repertoire.

Technology training helps promote technology innovations. These innovations result from a habit of collegial interactions: precise talk about implementing technology with instruction, feedback about that instruction, cooperative planning, and the sharing of technical knowledge with technology. For example, one Disney fourth-grade teacher was inspired to teach students how to develop interactive books. The interactive book *Parker and Penny* (Chapter 5, Figures 5.4 through 5.8) was one of several model projects that shaped the direction of technology skills for Grades 3 through 5.

The last and most important reason for training all staff is to guarantee that the technology program continues to move forward. When highly trained staff leave a school, the technology program often leaves with them. By continuing to train all staff to use technology, you ensure the technology program will not disintegrate. Often schools will hire a technology teacher or designate a technology specialist within the school. In these instances teachers have a tendency to turn over their instructional program to this specialist as they would to a physical education, art, or music teacher. However, when that specialist leaves, the technology program is often left with no one to carry the program forward. Training all staff protects the investment of technology and prevents the disintegration of the program.

Early Training at Walt Disney School

When the Disney staff committed themselves to technology in 1989, they decided that all teachers should be trained, especially if the school were spending the $25,000 acquired from State Supplemental Grant Funds. All teachers first participated in a 3-day summer training given by the Los Angeles County Office of Education on "Introduction to the Macintosh" and "Microsoft Works," the word processing program that had been selected (see Figure 8.2). County personnel came to the new Disney lab to train the staff (Figure 8.1).

After the training, teachers took the new computers home for summer practice. This proved to be a wise security move for the computers, especially during summer cleaning. When teachers arrived to begin school in the fall, 50% of the staff had practiced enough with the computers that they had prepared letters to parents and other teaching materials.

Although the teaching staff did not have any experience in working with a class in a computer lab situation, one of the fifth-grade teachers volunteered to begin using the lab even though the lab would accommodate only half of her students. This fifth-grade teacher took what she had learned through trial and error and prepared a written guide for other teachers. She used her guide to encourage and teach other teachers to use the lab with their students. Across the year, teachers began to bring their classes into the computer lab. Collaborative support was fostered as teachers began to share with each other, support one another, and depend on each other's expertise.

Also during that first year of implementation, local experts were trained among the staff in specific software programs to facilitate the student expectancy of improving student writing and publishing. Two teach-

Figure 8.1. Microsoft Works Training

MICROSOFT WORKS   FEE: $178

How to Use Word Processing, Spreadsheets, and Database (2-Day Class)

Participants will learn:

WORD PROCESSOR LESSONS

> Select, delete, restore, and move text.
> Change the appearance of text.
> Set margins and paragraph indents.
> Preview a word processor document before printing.
> Search and replace text.
> Use Works' dictionary to correct spelling errors.
> Use on-line help.
> Print a document.

DATABASE SKILLS

> Create a database document.
> Create database fields and set field attributes.
> Create a compound field.
> Enter and sort information.
> Create Selection Rules to view only certain records.
> Create a report and Print Preview a report.

SPREADSHEET SKILLS

> Create a new spreadsheet.
> Enter text, numbers, and formulas.
> Format cells to display dollars, dates, and percents.
> Change column widths.
> Create and remove cell notes.
> Create a pie chart.

PUTTING THE TOOLS TOGETHER—REPORTING AND PRINTING

> Draw and move lines, boxes, circles, and ovals.
> Change line thickness, fills, and patterns.
> Group and ungroup drawn objects.
> Copy and paste graphic objects within a word processor document.
> Copy a chart and paste it into a word processor document.
> Copy part of a spreadsheet document and paste it into a word processor form letter.
> Merge records from a database document into a word processor form letter.
> Create a word processor document to print mailing labels using information from a database document.
> (Participants are encouraged to bring a typical document that is currently being used in their classroom for use in the application exercise.)

PREREQUISITES: • Working knowledge of a typewriter keyboard.
                            • Introduction to the Macintosh course.

---

ers were trained in the use of PageMaker in order to publish the student newspaper. These teachers in turn trained students to write and publish the first school newspaper, *The Disney Chronicle*. This newspaper is published three times during the school year. Two other teachers were trained in the use of HyperStudio to use with students in the lab for curriculum projects. These local experts were not only empowered to use these programs with students, but to teach these programs to other teachers.

Technology training evolved from a commitment of 3 days during the summer to a continuous collaborative commitment in a variety of settings throughout 10 consecutive school years. At this writing, the emphasis on training all staff remains. As staff come and go, the culture and expectation that all teachers will learn to use technology remains at the forefront of what it means to be a teacher at Walt Disney School. This emphasis is reinforced and encouraged through a variety of collaborative training models.

Collaborative Training Models

We apply six collaborative training models in order to prepare our staff to use technology with students. The first model is called the *Focused Instruction Model*. In this model, teachers are trained to use specific technology skills in a classroom computer setting. This is the most common method of training teachers. The benefit of using this model is that it is time-effective and teachers learn specific skills related to a specific topic or software program. For example, in the first summer training of Disney staff, all teachers learned technology skills to use the basic word processing, spread sheet, and database programs in Microsoft Works.

The disadvantage of this method is that teachers have difficulty integrating their core curriculum with these technology skills. As a result, teachers have a tendency to see their curriculum and instruction as separate from the new technology skills learned. However, the focused instruction model is important because it is time-effective, providing a place to begin with new staff and a setting to update all staff on new software or hardware.

At Disney, the focused instruction model is used throughout the year. Prior to each school year, 2 or 3 days are set aside for training teachers new to the school in the basic operation of the computer lab, the student management program, and the word processing program, ClarisWorks (AppleWorks). Focused instruction also occurs on pupil free days and monthly after school on specific topics such as new software programs, use of multimedia, use of the Internet, and so on. Pupil free days in California are days set aside for staff development in which students don't come to school. Figure 8.2 is an example of Focused instruction given at the beginning of the school year.

Figure 8.2. Focused Instruction Sample

Attention All Teachers:

Monday, September 15, 1997

3:00 in the Computer Lab

Come to learn or refresh your memory on the skill of "Updating Your Workgroups" (AKA) deleting old students and adding new students to the At Ease Network.*

* You must do this before you can come into the lab with your class.

Small Group Collaboration is the second collaborative training model. In this model, teachers by grade level are trained to plan curriculum projects and to enhance them with technology. The great benefit to this model is that teachers link the grade-level curriculum to technology skills. Moreover, teachers, together, build support for risk taking and receive feedback on new innovative technology projects planned with their curriculum. The disadvantage is that only a small group of teachers is trained. However, the quality of the training addresses connecting the technology skills with the curriculum that the focused instruction formats can miss.

Teachers at a grade level or teachers new to Disney School are given substitutes once or twice a year so they can spend a morning planning technology with their curriculum. Instruction in the computer lab is also given; the projects are planned for before or after school or during other time intervals. Two site technology coordinators assist in training teachers to connect technology skills to their curriculum through the use of various software programs, of multimedia, and of the Internet. Figure 8.3 is an example of a survey given by the Disney technology specialists to plan training for teachers.

Peer Planning, Modeling, and Coaching is our third collaborative model in which a technology-skilled teacher works directly with one teacher to plan the curriculum and the technology project that will be completed with the class. The technology specialist models the first lesson for the teacher and his or her class in the computer lab. The regular classroom teacher observes the specialist teaching in the lab, then the regular teacher teaches the second lesson. While the regular teacher is teaching in the lab, the technology specialist observes. The specialist provides

Figure 8.3. Survey Sample

Teacher Technology Survey

Disney will be providing teachers with technology training that is necessary to help integrate classroom curriculum with the use of computers. Sessions will be held the last Monday of every month from 3:00-5:00 p.m. Participants will be paid for their time, and new teachers are strongly encouraged to attend. The first session will be on the Accelerated Reader Program for Grades 3, 4, and 5. This will be held on either Monday, January 26th, or Monday, February 2nd. Teachers will be notified.

We would like your input for the applications to be taught. Please identify your interest in any and all programs. Here are some suggestions, and if you think of others, please write them in (place tally marks under desired applications):

ClarisWorks   **Kid Pix/SuperPrint**

Netscape   **HyperStudio**

Write in your suggestions _____

_____

_____

_____

_____

_____

_____

_____

Thank you,
Susan and Jennifer

---

the teacher with coaching and feedback on the lesson after school. Teachers participate in analysis of the technology-enhanced curriculum project, including the skills taught and evaluation of the grade-level student expectancies achieved through actual work samples. The specialist also assists the teacher with planning of the next technology-enhanced curriculum project that builds on the previous project. The specialist will

Figure 8.4. Computer Assistance

Computer Assistance

Date: November 7, 1997
To: New Teachers
From: Jennifer
Re: Computer Demonstrations

Welcome to classroom technology! I'm sure that many, if not all, of you have had some computer experience. We have all come to realize that teaching computers to students is a whole different ball game. I am available to assist and demonstrate for you in the lab.

I have already given demo lessons to some of you, and I will be making follow-up visits as well. We need to schedule demonstrations for everyone in order to succeed with all students in the lab. I have the opportunity to be very flexible through the month of November into the first week of December.

Please let me know the next time you will be going into the lab and would like me to demonstrate or assist you. Here is the current schedule that I have:

Christin—Monday 9:15-10:15
Jennifer C.—Monday 12:15-1:15
Mike—Tuesday 10:30-11:30
Cris—Wednesday 12:30-1:30
Randi—Thursday 9:15-10:00
Louisa—Friday 10:30-11:30

If this is incorrect, please inform Susan or me to make the appropriate changes.

I am really looking forward to working with you and your classes!

Thank you!
Jennifer

---

continue to provide informal or formal assistance to the teacher as necessary throughout the year in integrating technology with the curriculum. Figure 8.4 is an example of how a Disney technology specialist organized peer planning, modeling, and coaching with new teachers.

This model is the most beneficial and effective way of helping a teacher to learn to use technology skills quickly with a class. Assistance is personalized and learning occurs quickly. However, we did find that the specialist must not only have technology skills, but also skills in observing and coaching and building rapport with teachers. The teachers who will be trained with this model must be open, willing to learn and to receive feedback.

There are disadvantages to this model. First, it limits the number of teachers who can be trained. If your school has a large staff, this model may not be practical and cost-effective, especially when considering the amount of planning time and release time for teachers. Second, you must have staff who can be coached. Some staff are highly resistant to any training. Other models may be more appropriate for resistant teachers; newer teachers are usually more open to this model. A trained technology specialist can be of great benefit to your new teachers in planning, implementing, and evaluating technology-enhanced projects.

At Disney School, we use this method of training primarily with newer teachers. Teachers are selected on a case-by-case basis in consultation with grade-level leaders and the principal. Technology specialists build rapport with these teachers at the beginning of the school year, during August technology training. This method has empowered teachers to become leaders at a given grade level or provide personnel for the next generation of technology specialists.

School Visitations is another collaborative training model that works well with staff, especially with highly resistant teachers. All teachers, or a selected group of teachers (including those who are resistant), visit a school with an advanced technology program. Getting staff out and away from their home school usually results in a new perspective on their own practices with technology. When teachers travel together, talk together, and eat lunch off site, their attitudes can be dramatically changed.

A school visitation made by the Disney leadership staff to an elementary school in the Covina Unified School District in 1990 helped in the decision to purchase open-ended software rather than tutorial software. This visit had a dramatic effect on future technology plans for software. In another visit to another elementary school in Los Angeles, Disney staff saw what was working and what wasn't working at the school. They had a chance to talk with teachers, students, and the principal. They formed opinions about how to configure the computers—in a lab or a classroom—as well as what hardware to purchase. The greatest benefit from these visits was that they helped to forge a unified vision for technology at Walt Disney School that was embraced by the staff rather than the principal alone.

When a school visitation is unstructured and the principal does not provide leadership, this model is ineffective as a means of training. The principal must lead a visitation by structuring it with a schedule, prearranging interactions with the host school, and then it is important that the principal lead the staff through the actual visitation. When leadership is absent, the visit can be a waste of time and can serve to diminish any vision for technology that exists. Often schools ask to visit Disney. One instance involved a school whose principal arrived an hour after her staff. Her late arrival sent a message to her school staff that the visitation was not important. However, when a school visitation is carefully structured and led by the school principal or assistant principal, the visit can be an effective means of motivating staff, especially in technology change.

The last collaborative training model is *Daily Problem Solving*. In technology, problem solving is ongoing. Designating teachers as technology specialists, grade-level technology leaders, or department technology leaders to work with teachers to solve problems in the computer lab or classroom is a necessity. Teachers can make the most complete plans and still have something go wrong with technology. Daily problem solving by designated staff will lower the anxiety of teachers when they are in the computer lab or classroom implementing instruction and will build collegial support in grade levels, departments, or both. Usually, problems that occur in the midst of instruction provide the most significant learning for teachers. Once a problem has occurred and has been solved with assistance, teachers gain confidence in their ability to solve technology problems while still knowing they have the support of other grade-level or department team members.

Teachers will tend not to use technology if they feel they have little assistance when implementing technology. The frustrations of having things go wrong with technology while managing an entire class is very threatening to a teacher's sense of teaching efficacy. Provision for designated staff or the principal to assist with daily problem solving will help teachers in implementing technology and building their own technology skills as they work with students.

Training all the staff at Disney has assisted daily problem solving. What one teacher doesn't know, another teacher does. Even with the limited time of staff, teachers know that they can call on other teachers in their grade level, the two technology specialists, or the principal for assistance in the computer lab or with use of classroom computers. Having problems with technology is approached as a normal by-product of technology. Teachers are not penalized for problems with technology but are encouraged and praised when they learn new skills and successfully overcome difficulties. The purpose of providing technology help is to empower teachers to the point where they develop expertise and can help others. This philosophy of training has served to promote ongoing technology expansion and development, even when trained staff leave the school.

The five collaborative training models developed at Walt Disney School assist all teachers to improve their use of technology. Specific models are used for distinct purposes. Focused training is a model that can be used with all staff for new instruction in software or specialized instruction in the use of hardware. Small group collaboration is especially effective for grade levels or departments. For example, Grades 3 and 4 use HyperStudio, whereas Grades 1 and 2 use SuperPrint. Training in grade levels individualizes training on specific software for use with the curriculum. Peer planning, modeling, and coaching is especially effective for newer teachers. It is highly personalized and instructive. This model is the most effective means of helping a teacher learn how to use technology skills with curriculum quickly. School visitations are particularly effective for resistant teachers and for forging a vision for staff. Finally, setting up a structure for daily problem solving can provide training in the everyday affairs of working with technology by offering support and encouragement for teachers as they learn technology skills needed at the moment.

Training Parents to Use Technology

Training parents as well as involving them in the development of a technology vision should be a priority at your school. In our experience, all parents support the development and use of technology with students. Through the Disney Parent Academy, parents are trained to use technology and are exposed to the same skills that their children are learning. Courses offered in the computer lab include basic word processing, publishing, and use of the Internet. These courses are offered during the evenings and are taught by Disney teachers. Parents participate in projects that teach basic technology skills that will support their children's learning (Figure 8.5).

Parent Academy classes also build rapport and support from the parents for the technology program. We have found that parents who attend Parent Academy classes participate more in school events and volunteer in the school. Further, these same parents become cheerleaders for a school's technology program and provide valuable input for yearly planning and program evaluation.

Budgeting for Training

Establishing a budget for training staff is the most important part of your overall technology budget. Often schools assume that training will occur automatically and never plan for the costs associated with arranging for teacher stipends, substitute costs, consultants, and workshops. At Disney School, 10% of the budget is set aside for training staff, as shown in the Disney Technology plan in Chapter 4. However, even 10% is sometimes not sufficient to meet the needs for training all staff.

Figure 8.5. Disney Parent Academy

Disney Parent Academy
Classes Offered Wednesday Evenings
May 7, 14, 21, 28

1. Introduction to ClarisWorks on the Computer

This class is a 4-week class for parents only. Parents will learn keyboarding skills, basic word processing, and publish a project by the end of the class. Spanish translation and babysitting will be available.

6:30-8:30 PM

2. Beginning ESL (English as a Second Language)

This class is a 4-week class for parents who do not speak English. Parents will practice basic spoken English.

6:30-8:30 PM

3. Skills for Positive Parenting

This class is a 4-week class for parents. Topics that will be covered include:

Week 1—The Art of Encouraging Your Child
Week 2—Communicating Effectively With Your Children
Week 3—Teaching Your Child Responsibility, Discipline, and Cooperation
Week 4—Helping Children With Study Skills

6:30-7:30 PM

REGISTRATION:

Each parent will need to register for the class. A babysitting/materials fee of $5.00 will be charged for each class so that parents will have the freedom to attend.

Disney Parent Academy

...Helping Parents Positively Affect the Lives of Children

PURPOSE:

The Disney Parent Academy is designed to provide classes for parents to assist in parenting and to strengthen and support the family structure of the home.

There are many additional ways to fund technology training. Accessing *free resources* is a means of extending the budget for training staff. District training, County Office of Education classes, and local colleges typically offer free or low-cost training for staff. Often, technology courses offered by educational organizations are very cost-effective. UCLA Extension rents the Disney computer lab for college courses. The rental money is used by Disney school for repairs and additional training. Grants are another means of funding training. Both federal and state grants always require training as a part of the grant application. Additionally, private corporations and businesses will sometimes supply personnel to assist with training. For example, a local computer repair business trains school staff to repair and maintain the computers at Disney. Whenever there is a difficult problem to solve, the repair technicians help to solve the problem solve and supply needed advice.

Planning for Training

A plan for technology training should be included in your school's technology plan. One of the best ways to organize technology training is to plan a yearly calendar. Divide the year into quarters or trimesters. Plan one trimester of training at a time. Include monthly training for all staff, grade levels, departments, and parents.

Planning must be flexible and adjust to the many demands of your school. Too often, the setting of a planning calendar leads to training that is inflexible and ceases to meet the needs of teachers and staff. There must be enough flexibility to allow for the many changes you know are going to occur in a public school. Technology training should not overwhelm teachers, especially when other demands are pressing. Your leadership team must be sensitive to the demands of classroom teaching and plan training for times when teachers can concentrate. Pupil free days or days when other demands are low should be considered. Figure 8.6 is an example of a pupil free training schedule.

The Disney plan includes monthly focused instruction sessions for either all staff or specific grade levels. Peer planning, modeling, and coaching is planned individually with selected teachers. Two Disney technology specialists lead the after-school sessions as well as the individualized training. These specialists also assist in training teachers through daily problem solving. The training topics are based on student expectancies and the needs of staff. Other local training from school district resources or local colleges is also incorporated into the calendar.

In this chapter, great emphasis has been placed on the training of all staff. The chief advantage of training everyone is that when trained staff leave the school, the technology program will remain. Also, training all

Figure 8.6. Computer Inservice Schedule

MARCH 1, 1996

COMPUTER INSERVICE SCHEDULE

All teachers and instructional assistants are welcome to participate in the training during their regularly scheduled hours or the entire day.

TIME	SOFTWARE	PROJECT	TEACHER
8:30-10:00	SUPERPRINT	Making a poster	Dawn
10:15-11:45	CLARISWORKS	Using the spreadsheet Graphing	Susan
11:45-12:45	LUNCH—LUNCH—LUNCH—LUNCH—LUNCH—LUNCH		
1:00-2:00	ACTION	Making a multimedia presentation	Pat
2:00-3:00	HYPERSTUDIO	Making a slide show	Dianne

PLEASE CONTACT PAT FOR ANY SPECIAL SESSIONS USING THE DIGITAL QUICKTAKE CAMERA, OR PREPARING A SLIDE SHOW, ETC.

---

staff helps to build collaborative support for risk taking. When a high degree of collaboration exists within a staff, innovative technology practices are fostered. Six collaborative models used at Walt Disney School have been discussed. Through these collaborative training models, collaborative support has been developed and, as a result, the Disney technology program has continued to grow and develop over the years.

9

CHAPTER

Management of the Technology Environment

....

On any day, and certainly when you are least expecting it, a disaster can occur with technology. This disaster may be a frozen computer, a printer that won't print, a computer that displays a sad face and makes a mournful cry, an error message on the screen that no one understands, a computer that can't find the file server, as well as many other sad scenarios. These are common problems that can and do occur when teachers use technology with students. Any of these problems can create great anxiety and discourage teachers from using technology at all. Since problems will most certainly occur, every school needs a management plan for its technology program.

That management plan must be concerned with establishing a technology response team to respond to the needs of teachers. Schedules for student and teacher training will need to be organized. The local area network (LAN) and computers must be maintained by school site personnel to guarantee that students will have access to the technology. Periodically, memory for these computers will need to be upgraded as software is improved. Schools must have a repair plan in place with the District or local businesses for any parts that need to be replaced. Finally, the management plan must include some form of evaluation so that technology can be improved from year to year. Establishing a management plan will not stop all technology disasters from occurring, but it will provide resources for classroom teachers and students using the tools of technology with the curriculum.

The Role of the Principal

The role of the principal is key in establishing a technology management plan. The principal's role is one of leadership for technology. This leadership does not mean merely delegating to a local expert the responsibilities, planning, and change that technology demands so that the principal can concentrate on other priorities.

Leadership for technology involves a principal's willingness to become schooled in technology; specifically, learning the use of a computer and gaining a basic understanding of networking in order to plan for the short- and long-term changes at the school site.

Second, a principal's leadership is necessary to lead staff through the stress of the change demanded by technology. If staff do not feel that the principal is with them, they may feel that the change is not worth their effort or is not important to the school. As with any major change, the principal is critical in minimizing stress during implementation, providing feedback on how well the change is going, evaluating the program, and establishing a vision for where the next technology changes will occur.

A principal's leadership is also necessary to lead staff through technology challenges. There will be many challenges, such as struggles with deteriorating buildings, staff resistant to training, funding, the slow bureaucratic processes in districts, and so on. If the principal's leadership is absent in these times of challenge, technology change will not be successfully implemented.

A principal's leadership style is critical with respect to how the principal responds to staff needs when using technology. Staff must feel supported or they will not risk using technology. This does not mean the principal must solve every technology problem a teacher may have in the computer lab or classroom, but that organizational processes are in place to assist teachers. Only the principal can provide that leadership.

The Role of the Site Technology Team

Your site Technology Team is a team organized by the principal representing all faculty and staff to assist in the management of technology at the school. This team will address several areas:

- Planning the personnel who will respond when a problem occurs in the classroom or computer lab
- Scheduling the use of technology resources for the greatest student access
- Scheduling ongoing training for staff, and complete general network maintenance
- Ordering hardware and software
- Updating software and reformatting system software
- Installing hardware and software
- Locating community/District support for hardware and maintenance

- Budgeting for repairs
- Evaluating student results
- Updating the school technology plan yearly

Your site technology team should meet at least once a month to solve problems and to plan and coordinate these activities.

Responding to Emergencies

At Disney School, two site technology specialists, the principal, the curriculum lab assistant, and the custodian respond to emergencies with technology. The technology specialists are teachers who are trained and receive a yearly stipend. Since the technology specialists are also classroom teachers, coverage for their classes is provided when the problem is severe. For example, there are often printing problems and frozen computers. A member of the emergency team will help the teacher to address these issues while the teacher is teaching her class. Because all classroom teachers are trained, other teachers provide a back-up support system for teachers. If the problem is severe, such as a file server going down, the District Technology Coordinator will intervene immediately. At times the computer lab will not be accessible, depending on the problem.

Scheduling

Scheduling students in the computer lab is always a challenge. Teachers always request more time for students in the computer lab than exists. The technology team at Disney decided that greater access and more time would be given to Grades 3 through 5 because of the complexity of their projects. Blocks of 1½ hours are scheduled for third- through fifth-grade students twice a week. Grades K through 2 students meet at least 1½ hours once a week (Figure 9.1). Still, Disney teachers feel that this is not enough time. The challenge is to provide more computers and the same kind of access to technology tools as to paper and pencils.

Another Tech Team function is to schedule ongoing training. The focused instruction model is scheduled once a month on various topics; meetings are held after students are dismissed. Teachers are also sent away from the school site for specific training, to garner specific expertise, and they in turn help teachers implement technology instruction with students. Grade-level collaborative training for grade levels is focused on the needs of grade levels; for example, Grades 3 through 5 recently participated in training for Accelerated Reader, a reading program for students. The peer modeling and coaching collaborative training model is scheduled informally with new teachers and individual teachers as needed.

Figure 9.1. Computer Schedule

Computer Schedule
1998-1999

Monday	Tuesday	Wednesday	Thursday	Friday
8:15-9:15 Pat		8:15-9:15 Betty		
8:30-9:30 alt. Yelena/Dianne/ Christin		8:45-9:45 Nien		8:45-9:45 Louisa
	9:15-10:15 Lisa/Vicki		9:15-10:00 Randi	
9:30-10:30 Lori		9:45-10:30 alt. Bridget/Terry/Jennifer		9:45-10:30 alt. Roberta/Lori/Jennifer
	10:25-11:25 Judy			
11:00-12:00 Bridget		11:00-12:30 Roberta	11:00-12:30 Dianne	11:00-12:00 Christin
12:15-1:15 Teresa	12:00-1:00 Amy	12:30-1:30 Cris	12:30-1:30 Leatrice	12:15-1:15 Melissa
1:30-3:00 Terry	1:00-2:00 Anita	1:30-3:00 Jennifer	1:30-3:00 Yelena	1:30-3:00 Jennifer
	Early dismissal			

Group problem solving is the most informal method of training and occurs daily among teachers. In this kind of training, teachers learn as they use technology with the curriculum. Overall, the Tech Team monitors and guides the growth of technology training with teachers so that student expectancies in the technology plan may be achieved.

General Network Maintenance

General network maintenance refers to the care of the file server, computers, printers, cables, and hubs in the local area network (LAN). Cables are checked to see that they are in good condition and are securely connected to all devices in the LAN. The file server will need to be "backed up" daily to an external (or internal) hard drive so that all files have a duplicate copy. Installing an automated back-up system for a file server is a necessity for any LAN. Back-up systems should be automated every day to back up work that is completed during that day. Printers will need ink cartridges, paper, and periodic cleaning of rubber feeder rollers. Computer screens, keyboards, and mice that are used by many students and staff will need to be cleaned at least once per week. In addition, old files will periodically need to be taken off the file server by teachers so that hard drive space can be freed for other projects.

When system software becomes corrupt, or loses its ability to function properly with programs such as Microsoft Word, the hard drives of computers will need to be reformatted. Problems such as a frozen computer, error messages, lack-of-memory messages, a slowing down of computer functions, and other strange problems could signal the need for putting on new system software.

The Tech Team is responsible for putting on fresh system software and application software when computers begin to have problems with freezing or experience unusual behaviors. Some of these problems can be diagnosed through the use of Norton Utilities or Disk First Aide programs. There are more than 70 computers at Disney, and these utility programs often cannot fix issues related to the hard drive. Every Tech Team should have training in reformatting computer hard drives with fresh system software on a rotational basis. When problems accumulate and computer workstations are dysfunctional, student access is immediately curtailed.

Software and Memory Upgrades

Computers will also need periodic memory upgrades, especially as the memory requirements for software change. Not only will system software requirements change (Windows 95 to Windows 98, for example) but application software as well (MS Word 5.0 to MS Word 6.0, etc.). With these continual software upgrades, there will always be a demand for additional memory and hard drive space. These needs will need to be budgeted into any technology plan.

Newer computers may not be compatible with older software. For example, when the Disney lab was upgraded to 96 mg of RAM (random-access memory), half of the computers in the lab were Macintosh G3 computers. The ClarisWorks, Kid Pix, and SuperPrint programs had to be upgraded (the most recent software secured) due to these newer computers. The Tech Team is responsible for managing these kinds of ongoing changes.

Developing a Repair Plan

One of the best community partnerships a school can form is with a local computer repair business. Thanks to a local business close to Disney School, advice, counsel, and repairs are easily accomplished. The owners of such repair businesses can provide support to Tech Teams in diagnosing specific problems with networking related to a LAN or for general computer maintenance. Often our business partner is able to assist Disney with specific problems, which helps save our school money in needless repairs. In addition, through this business partnership, the Disney Tech Team continually learns more about the maintenance of the technology program and the new technology coming out on the market.

The need for repairs will undoubtedly occur. Therefore, the school must have a plan for repairs. Having District hardware and software specialists is helpful as a first line of defense. However, Disney School shares the demand for these personnel with 16 other Burbank schools. Formulating a partnership with a computer repair business as well as training Tech Team members to make simple repairs has helped us fix faulty computers quickly. As a result, Tech Team staff have become well trained in diagnosing problems rather than waiting for weeks for computers to be fixed.

Evaluating the Technology Program

Evaluating the technology plan is another important function of the Tech Team. Through the collaborative teaming process, site technology coordinators evaluate the plan and make recommendations for improvement. These recommendations are brought to the Leadership Team, which monitors student progress toward expectancies for the overall technology program. Based upon actual student work and projects where technology has been integrated into the curriculum, improvement is recommended and the technology plan revised.

All of the functions of the site technology team are critically important to the advancement of technology at your school. Without this support, management, and organization in place, technology change will not be sustained over time.

Technology Security Issues

The security and use of technology must be protected, and there are several important security issues that you must address. The first and most obvious is that of facility security to protect your investment. When a computer lab was first established at Disney, one of the first security recommendations was to replace the doors of the classroom planned for the lab. Steel doors with deadbolt locks were recommended as one of the first security precautions. A second recommendation was to put the lab in an interior classroom where it would be difficult for theft to occur. Obtaining an alarm system was the third recommendation. An alarm system allows us to have the lab monitored through a security service that contacts the police department when the alarm sounds. Other security recommendations include engraving computers and securing them to tables. Fortunately, District personnel were able to facilitate these security issues for our school. However, all of these measures should be considered by schools to secure technology equipment.

Not only must physical security be planned but also *access* security. Determining who will have access to files must be considered. For example, students should never have access to the file server administration files. Student and teacher files must be managed in such a way as to guarantee both security and storage. Management software such as Apple's Mac Manager program not only controls the security and storage of our files but also access to the applications, printers, and removable media students will use. At Ease also denies unauthorized persons access to the file server and other critical files necessary to the effective functioning of the file server and workstations.

Where the Internet is concerned, you must control access to inappropriate sites through screening software or a *firewall.* A firewall is a computer that is programmed to screen out inappropriate Internet addresses. In our District, a dedicated computer with a firewall screens out inappropriate Internet sites for all 17 schools. However, for schools without a firewall, screening software must be purchased. Common Internet screening software programs include: NetNanny, Cyber Patrol, SurfWatch, and CYBERsitter. A complete listing of Internet blocking software Web sites is included in Resource A. This software is commonly ordered for each workstation with an Internet address. The school can either take the responsibility for screening out inappropriate sites through a program like NetNanny or allow a program like Cyber Patrol to make the decisions regarding what Internet sites to block. Cyber Patrol sends weekly upgrades of inappropriate sites via Internet address to specific computers. Either way, you will need to decide how the Internet must be screened for inappropriate sites to quell the worries of parents.

With Internet use you must also be concerned about viruses that are transmitted through the Internet, e-mail, or disks coming into the school from students or staff. Virus protection software is a necessity for all your computers. Norton's Anti-Virus Protection or other virus protection programs are necessary to protect computers. Normally, this software is sold and licensed for each workstation ($20 per workstation).

Security issues related to technology are important to address at any school. One principal in a neighboring district, after spending months raising money for computers, lost them all in one evening's raid on the school. Plans must be made in advance not only to secure your technology equipment but also to protect students from potentially harmful information through the Internet or e-mail. Planning is the best preventative maintenance your Tech Team can do.

Extending Technology to Parents

Parents can and should be your school's best partners for technology. Regardless of the kind of school, parents are always in favor of technology for their children. When Disney first began its technology program in 1990, key parents were also trained in the use of technology, especially the PTA officers responsible for programs at the school. These parents became cheerleaders for the technology program in the first few years of implementing technology. In the early 1990s, Disney did not have Title 1 funds and had very few funds due to a small enrollment. The PTA became a supportive advocate in assisting the technology program through fund-raisers and their own use of technology for bulletins, newsletters, and yearbooks developed with the technology at the school. Empowering parents became an important part of our technology growth.

Training was later expanded to the general parent population through the Disney Parent Academy. Figure 8.5 in Chapter 8 is an example of a brochure offered to parents. Courses were provided in the general use of the computer. Parents participated in learning basic word processing and published several projects using the computer. Training continues, with the Parent Academy offering 4-week courses to parents during fall, winter, and spring of each year. Disney teachers volunteer to serve as teachers for these courses. As a result of parents participating in these classes and other Parent Academy classes, parent participation overall has increased in the school.

Internet dial-up and homework access is another way for parents to maintain communication and contact with the school. Once an Internet LAN has been established, dial-up access is not difficult and can be provided for parents. When teachers are trained to post homework and parents have access through home computers, this can be a regular form of access. Currently, Disney has a dial-up system that teachers can access from home, and parent access is an area that is being developed. Since Internet access has been developed, the Disney Web page is another means of posting information for parents and students, and for parents to access information about the school.

Summary

Technology is an effective tool for schools to improve the learning of their students. Where technology is integrated into the curriculum and not considered as a separate discipline or used solely as a means for drill and practice of skills, technology has been shown to be very effective. Research by Wenglinsky (1998) and others has shown that using technology tutorials that emphasize drill and practice has little effect on learning. However, when technology is used as a tool that causes the student to think and apply concepts from the curriculum, learning is improved.

This book has attempted to provide school leaders with a process for setting up a successful technology program that improves learning at schools. The first step is preparation of the school environment for technology change. This can be accomplished through lead management. Lead management will foster the development of a collaborative school team. Collaborative teams, in turn, provide a support structure for the dynamic changes that technology will bring.

Allowing student expectancies to guide the use of technology is the second important step in integrating technology. What we want for our students must always guide our decisions for technology. Organizing the curriculum through concept-based instruction will encourage students to apply knowledge to real-world situations. Technology skills integrated in a concept-based curriculum not only elevate thinking levels but also provide a meaningful context for learning.

Designing a useful, dynamic plan is the third important step. This plan must articulate the mission and expectancies for students as well as connect technology skills with an integrated curriculum. Based on these expectancies and curriculum focus, the networking plan and selections for hardware and software can be made. Staff training becomes a logical step toward implementing these expectancies for students. The management structure assists teachers' implementation of technology and guarantees ongoing access for staff and students. Finally, evaluating student progress toward expectancies becomes a collaborative process that occurs throughout the year until the technology plan is again revised.

These steps are revisited each year in order to bring about steady improvement in the overall technology program. This process is never static and continues to change through ongoing examination by staff. By implementing these steps, your school can build and expand a technology program that will directly affect student achievement for years to come.

Web Site URLs

Search Engines

http://www.yahoo.com	Yahoo
http://yahooligans.com/	Yahooligans! Web Guide for Kids
http://sunsite.unc.edu/cisco/schoolhouse.html	Virtual Schoolhouse
nckinley.com	Magellan
tavista.digital.com	Alta Vista
ler.com/	Web Crawler
mu.edu/	Lycos

Museums

http://www.emf.net/louvre/	Louvre Online
http://www.si.edu	Smithsonian Institute
http://artsednet.getty.edu	Getty Museum DBEA Art Program
http://sln.fi.edu	Franklin Institute Science Museum
http://www.namaa.si.edu/	National Museum of American Art (NMAA)

Government Agency Sites

http://www.whitehouse.gov	The White House Web site
http://www.nara.gov	National Archives and Records
http://www.whitehouse.gov/WH/kids/html/home.html	The White House For Kids
http://lcweb.loc.gov/h21omepage/lchp.html	The Library of Congress
http://www.ed.gov/	U.S. Department of Education

Computer Hardware/Software

http://www.apple.com	Apple Computer Web site
http://www.ibm.com	IBM Computer Web site
http://www.microsoft.com	Microsoft Software
http://www.adobe.com	Adobe Software
http://www.hp.com/	Hewlett-Packard Web site

Internet Blocking Sites

http://www.netnanny.com/	NetNanny
http://www.cyberpatrol.com/	Cyber Patrol
http://www.cybersitter.com/	CYBERsitter
http://www.pearlsw.com/	Cyber Snoop
http://www1.surfwatch.com/	SurfWatch
http://www.FamilyConnect.com/	Family Connect
http://www.surfcontrol.com/	Surf Control
http://www.securitysoft.com/	Cyber Sentinel

http://www.webchaperone.com/   Web Chaperone

Web Page/HTML References

http://www.emerson.emory.edu/services.html/   HTML Authors Toolkit
html.html

http://www.chem.emory.edu/html/html.html   The Complete Guide to HTML

http://www.zeldman.com/faq.html   Ask Dr. Web

Math/Science Web Sites

http://sln.fi.edu/   Franklin Institute's Science Learning Network

http://www.bev.net/education/SeaWorld/   Sea World
homepage.html

http://seds.lpl.arizona.edu/nineplanets/   The Nine Planets
nineplanets/nineplanets.html

http://www.cs.yale.edu/HTML/YALE/CS/   The Froggy Page
HyPlans/loosemore-sandra/froggy/html

http://www.c3.lanl.gov:80/mega-math/   Mega Math

http://www.nasa.gov/nasa_online_   NASA Online Educ.Resources
education.html

http://spacelink.msfc.nasa.gov/   NASA Spacelink

http://www.nsf.gov/   National Science Foundation

http://mwanal.lanl.gov/CST/imagemap/periodic/   Periodic Table of the Elements
periodic.html

http://rampages.onramp.net/~jaldr/chemtchr.   Chemistry Teacher Resources
html

http://www.hcc.hawaii.edu/dinos/dinos.1.html   Dinosaur Exhibit

http://www.gps.caltech.edu/~polet/recofd.   Caltech's Earthquake of the Day
html

http://www.aapt.org/	American Association of Physics Teachers
http://ranier.oact.hq.nasa.gov/Sensors_page/Planets.html	Planetary Tour Guide
http://quest.arc.nasa.gov/	Quest: NASA's K-12 Internet Initiative
http://www.usgs.gov/education/	U.S. Geological Survey Web
http://cirrus.sprl.umich.edu/wxnet/	Weather Net
http://www.cchem.berkeley.edu/Table/index.html	WebElements (Periodic Table)

History/Social Science

http://www.cnn.com	CNN News Network
http://socialstudies.com:80/index.html	Social Studies School Service
http://www.pbs.org	Public Broadcasting System
http://www.discovery.com	Discovery Channel
http://www.odci.gov/cia/publications/97fact/index.html	CIA World Factbook
http://sln.fi.edu/franklin/rotten.html	The World of Benjamin Franklin
http://www.historychannel.com/today	This Day in History
http://funnelweb.utcc.utk.edu/~Ehoemann/warweb.html	The American Civil War Home Page

Internet Glossary

··

A

address

An address is the unique identifier you need either (a) to access the services of an Internet site or (b) to send e-mail. Another word for Internet site addresses is URL (see URL). E-mail addresses are in the form of user name@server.com and provide a unique identifier for your in-box so your mail can find you.

analog

Analog is an adjective used to describe things that are continuous. Think of the two types of stereo system volume control for comparison. With some, turning to raise or lower volume is smooth. With others, as you turn, the knob clicks into several stops between low and high; there's no setting in between. The smooth turning is analog, offering infinite variations between 1 and 10. The digital side offers only 10 choices, but is highly accurate.

anonymous FTP

Anonymous FTP uses the FTP (link) protocol to allow many users access to a set of files. Users can log into an anonymous FTP site using the login name "anonymous." With regular FTP, the user needs a system name and password to access the site. Anonymous FTP sites usually contain public domain software or data, free for the taking.

AOL

AOL stands for America Online, a leading online service. America Online provides Internet access plus a number of member services, such as news, special-interest areas, and virtual chat rooms.

Archie

Despite the appearance of "Veronica" (link) in this same glossary, Archie refers not to the well-known comic-book character, but to a collection of software tools used to search for information stored on anonymous FTP sites. There is also a Jughead services that lets you search for Gopher links.

ARPANET

ARPANET (which stands for Advanced Research Projects Agency Network) is a wide-area network of government- and university-based computers that was started in the early 1960s. ARPANET eventually spawned the Internet, but it would be decades before the bulk of the users showed up—not to mention the myriad businesses wishing to ride the internetworking wave to big profits. The U.S. Department of Defense originally planned ARPANET as a computer network that, because it was distributed across the country, could survive a nuclear war. Unfortunately, the creators of ARPANET could not foresee the high-bandwidth needs of today's users, which have caused some to call for a revamping of the Internet's structure.

ASCII

ASCII files or "plain text format" files are text (letters and numbers and punctuation) that's free of any special formatting such as boldface, italics, or fancy formatting. Every computer can open an ASCII file, and almost every word-processing program can make and save ASCII files. The simplest word-processing programs (such as Notepad, for Windows users) use only ASCII and don't add any specialized commands or codes.

B

backbone

A backbone is any central portion of a communications network where many lines come together. Backbones are designed to transport huge volumes of data before distributing them back down regional phone lines to your computer. Think of an interstate highway. If you need to make a long trip, you take a small road from your house to a bigger road, then take bigger and bigger roads until you hit the interstate, where you can travel much more quickly. When you get close to your destination, you take a series of smaller roads again until you get where you're going. A backbone is made up of hardware such as relays and switches in addition to high-bandwidth communications lines.

bandwidth

In practice, bandwidth how you describe how much data you can stuff over a single connection in a given time. (See bps for the yardstick used.) In technical terms, it's the difference (measured in hertz) between the high and low frequencies of the connection. Unfortunately, you don't usually hear the word *bandwidth* bandied about unless you don't have enough of it. While 14.4 or 28.8 bps does fine for sending text, still pictures, and the occasional sound file, for routine full-motion video downloads, an ISDN line (link) only begins to solve the bandwidth issues you face.

baud

Sometimes you hear baud tossed about as a synonym for bits per second, or bps (link)—as in, "That system's modem is only 9,600 baud." Be warned: While the two can be synonymous, that's not always the case. Baud technically refers to how frequently a modem's signal shifts value, which, depending on the bps-class of modem, could be once per transmitted bit or once after transmitting several bits. While this is probably more than you ever needed to know about the word *baud*, to avoid making a technical misstep, always use "bps" when talking about modem or network speed.

BBS

BBS stands for Bulletin-Board System, a network comprising one or more PCs, equipped with modems and special communications software, that are set up for the purpose of taking calls from subscribers. When subscribers call in, they can navigate the system to talk to other users or download information. While they are fading from popularity now, due to the Internet and the World Wide Web, BBSs were the main source of online community for many years. The main drawback to BBSs is that you have to dial in over a normal phone line.

Binary

Binary means something with two parts. Computers use a binary language composed of ones and zeros to do things and talk to other computers. All your files, for instance, are kept in the computer as binary files and translated into words and pictures by the software (which is also, yes, ones and zeros). Most of the files you'll create with word processors, spreadsheets, and graphics packages are kept in a binary form that certain software can understand and other software can't, so if you need to use such a file you'll have to have the right software to interpret it. Some files that use only simple letters and numbers and no special formatting are created in a format called ASCII, which uses a small set of binary codes that all software interprets the same.

BinHex

More than a curse placed on various stored food or objects, this term refers to a way of converting a binary file into ASCII characters. Why bother? It's very easy to transmit ASCII text over the Internet, but it can be more complex to transmit binary files. A BinHex conversion provides a stepping stone. If you want to send a program to a friend, you can convert it first into BinHex format, then send it to your friend who converts it back. BinHex files usually take up more space than their non-BinHexed counterparts. Most compression utilities such as StuffIt and PKZIP can convert and deconvert BinHex files.

bookmark

A bookmark is a place holder to a particular URL, or Web address, that you set once in your Internet browser software for ready access later. Bookmarks are typically used to record a site you want to return to, or one you visit regularly.

bps

bps stands for Bits Per Second, the measure of a modem's signaling speed. However, the only term you'll hear describing new modems is Kbps, for kilo bits per second—as in 28.8 Kbps, meaning 28,800 bits per second.

broadband

Broadband, also called wideband, refers to any communications channel that can carry signals with multiple frequencies. Broadband communications, as a result, permit several independent signals to travel across a single cable simultaneously without getting into each other's way. The term is commonly used to describe the much-touted and eagerly awaited high-speed access lines of the future.

Browser

Browser is the generic term for any piece of software that lets you see Web pages. You may use the Netscape Navigator browser (currently the most popular browser in the world), or perhaps you use the Microsoft Internet Explorer browser or America Online. The very first Web browsers, such as Lynx, allowed users to see only the text of Web pages. Mosaic was the first browser to introduce graphics.

Buffer

The buffer in your computer acts as a kind of holding tank for information while it waits for you to need that info. As you might have guessed, you and your computer work at very different speeds. Moreover, you gather information differently: Where humans read one word after the other, one by one, a computer tends to scoop up one chunk of data, then another, then another. If your computer has a fair amount of memory devoted to acting as a data buffer, your programs will probably run more smoothly, since the computer won't constantly have to replenish what's in its tiny holding tank.

C

cache

Have you noticed that once you've visited a particular Web page, if you click to it again it usually appears on screen faster? That's your cache at work. A cache is an area of your computer's memory or its hard drive that stores Web text and images you've already seen. When your browser asks to see those things again, the computer has them on hand and doesn't have to get them from the Net. Once you're done using the Web for the day, the cache automatically gets dumped like a big trash can.

carrier

A carrier is any computer with which you've established a connection. On an external modem (or an internal one whose software graphically mimics an external one) the CD light (which predates compact discs) stands for Carrier Detect; it lights up when your computer and the other one (the carrier) have made a connection. Should the connection drop for any reason, your communications software may display a "no carrier" or "dropped carrier" message, both of which mean the same thing in practical terms: You must reconnect.

case-sensitive

Case-sensitive refers to whether or not a given software program, or a communications protocol such as IP, requires you to type with strict attention to upper- and lower-case characters. If a program sees the letters "UPS" and "ups" as the same, it is not case-sensitive. If it sees them as different, then it is.

client

Picture the Web as a business, with yourself as the client. You ask the Web for certain services and the Web provides them. Now just substitute the word *server* for *business*, and you'll understand client/server communications. Client software interprets the information servers send out. Your browser (and most other Internet applications for that matter: e-mail, FTP, Telnet, etc.) is a piece of client software. Clients sent queries to various servers on the Internet for information. The servers serve the information to your computer, where your client software interprets it. In other words, client software handles sending and receiving on your end, server software sends and receives on the Internet's end. Unless you're an Internet service provider, chances are every piece of software you use for exploring the Web is a client.

command line

Any area of a screen, in certain software, that lets you key in commands, preferably in whatever format that software requires. DOS, which appears only in a cameo for most users of Windows 95, is a prime example of a command line interface. UNIX, the operating system running on thousands of Internet servers, is another good example. Graphical user interfaces such as those found in Windows and Macintosh software largely dispense with command lines through the extensive sue of menus, dialog boxes, and other shortcuts. Proponents of command-line interfaces often argue that they offer the user far more control over the computer. Detractors point out that they are next to impossible to use if you don't know a lot about computers.

compression

Any of various ways of squeezing a file down to a smaller size. Compressed files save you time because they transfer much more quickly. Software that compresses files, such as the shareware utility PKZIP.EXE, or StuffIt, looks for repetition in the bytes comprising a file and assigns various codes that represent the repeated bytes—without storing the actual bytes in the file's compressed version. Another form of compression, disk compression, refers to software that compresses all data on a given hard disk.

CompuServe

CompuServe was once the largest online service, but in recent years it has dropped a notch thanks to America Online, the world's foremost practitioner of floppy-disk philanthropy. CompuServe offers a variety of news, entertainment, and special-interest services, not to mention Internet access.

cookie

If you've ever wandered around a Web shopping mall throwing goodies into a virtual shopping cart, you've been making Web cookies. A cookie is a small piece of information that a Web server (such as the one that holds the Web shopping mall) sends to your browser to hold onto until it's time for the server to read it. For instance, the cookie made while you shop around a Web mall contains a list of the items you're planning to purchase. When you head to the checkout desk, the server collects the cookie from your browser to see what you're buying. Cookies also have expiration dates and instructions about which sites can "eat" them, along with security information to protect your buying info.

cracker

Cracker is a word created by the hacker community in the mid-1980s to describe someone who tries to break into a computer system by cracking passwords. The difference between hackers and crackers (other than the competing, too-pat definition of honest vs. dishonest) is one of technical prowess: Hackers—malicious ones—break into systems through their sheer intelligence and mastery of the technologies involved. According to hackers, crackers break into the same systems through a little bit of knowledge and a whole lot of luck.

cross-posting

This is the practice of posting a message in more than one Internet news group, done when the message's creator believes the topic worthy of interest to more than one news group. Cross-posting can be rewarding when the message's creator is selective enough to post the message only where appropriate, and not in a way that arrogantly blankets myriad news groups.

cyberpunk

Cyberpunk started as a sub-genre of science-fiction novels by William Gibson and Bruce Sterling in the late 1970s and early 1980s, works that combined elements of cyberspace with darkness and a nihilistic "punk" attitude. From there it has evolved into a lifestyle encompassing clothing, music, outlook, and technology.

cyberspace

Cyberspace is the all-encompassing word for the space created by electronic communications, originally from the William Gibson novel *Necromancer.* It includes all the available resources we find on the Internet: information and entertainment.

D

daemon

A daemon is a program that lurks in the background of a computer's operation, stepping in to do specific functions that the user hasn't explicitly commanded but nevertheless needs done. A daemon on an Internet server, for instance, might be responsible for authorizing client log-ons, or for routing incoming e-mail to the correct user.

dial-up

Dial-up describes the kind of connection you have if you dial a number through your computer to connect to your ISP. Dial-up differentiates standard phone line connections from other, higher speed lines that maintain a constant connection between two points, such as T1 lines.

digital

Digital signifies something that has only two states, 1 and 0. The difference between analog (link) and digital is the difference between a light bulb controlled by a dimmer and one controlled by an on/off switch. Of course, your computer is digital, and it needs a lot more information than just a 1 or a 0 to keep it running. It uses digital information, made up of a complex series of 1s and 0s, to get the job done.

dither

The process by which the browsers try to make their very few colors compensate for so many colors is called dithering. The browsers create an approximate version of the color they don't have, sort of like mixing paint in an understocked paint store. Sometimes it succeeds, and sometimes it doesn't.

DNS

Ever wondered how your Internet connection knows exactly where to find all the places you tell it to go? A computer called a DNS handles the map-reading duties for you on the Internet. When you type in or click on a URL, it gets sent to the DNS to figure out where the URL might be located and finds it. DNS stands for Domain Name Server.

domain

The last part of an Internet site's domain name tells what kind of site it is. The most rapidly expanding of these is .com, as in www.cnn.com. Other common ones include .edu, for educational institutions; .gov for government; and .mil, for military sites. For sites based outside the United States, there are many others.

domain name

A domain name is the last two parts of an Internet address. For instance, the URL for Yahoo begins with www.yahoo.com. The "www" part tells the server the machine from which you'd like to retrieve information. Some sites, however, have no precursor at all, such as Netscape: home.netscape.com.

download

Online, you can get software by downloading it. The software sits on Computer X; you use your browser or an FTP (file-transfer protocol) program to find the software and retrieve it to your computer. If you had software you wanted to send to another computer, you'd reverse the process; this is known as uploading.

E

e-mail

E-mail is electronic mail. It's the digital, packetized means of transmitting messages via phone lines to other people's computers using an online service or ISP.

encryption

Computer telecommunications are notoriously insecure. Because of this fact, if you want to transmit something you don't want anyone else to see (such as credit card information, passwords, or trade secrets), you have to use one of the variety of encryption schemes that convert files into a secret code before transmission. At the other end, if all is well, your intended recipient's software will decrypt it for use. The most secure form of encryption available right now is called public key encryption. Everyone using this system has two keys, a public key (available to the public) and a private key (to be kept secret). If Person A wants to send Person B a document, Person A encodes it using person B's public key. Once it's been encoded, only Person B's private key can decode it.

Ethernet

Ethernet is the dominant scheme for networking PC-level computers and related hardware. Developed by Xerox, Digital, and Intel, Ethernet initially lets you transmit files and data at 10 megabits per second, or 10 million bps. The many competing versions of the newer Fast Ethernet, however, go 10 times that speed. Most office networks use Ethernet, which is why they are usually faster than your dial-up line at home.

extension

PCs use file extension—a dot (period) and two, three, or four letters—at the end of file names to keep track of what kind of file it is. For instance, Microsoft Word files usually have a .doc extension, while Web pages that use Hypertext Markup Language have an .htm or .html extension. Older PCs running Windows 3.11 or DOS can't handle extensions with more than three letters. On the other hand, Macintoshes understand so well that Mac users don't have to use or see extensions at all. Recognizing file extensions helps you when you're trying to figure out something your browser has found but can't understand. Netscape users can see a list of the extensions their browser knows about by clicking on Options (for 2.0 users), then General Preferences, then Helpers. As you add plug-ins to your browser, you'll find yourself making changes to the Options list and its set of known extensions.

F

404

When your browser can't find a page that you've asked for or that it isn't allowed to let you have, your browser will display a page that says, "404 Error: File Not Found." If you get this message, there's nothing to do but back up and try another link.

fiber-optic cable

Fiber-optics is a technology that permits digitized voice and data to travel as beams of light—rather than as electrical impulses—along the microthin strands of glass that make up a fiber-optic cable. Theoretically, communication along fiber-optic cable flashes along at the speed of light.

It's also high bandwidth (link), permitting data to travel at roughly 45 megabits a second.

finger

An Internet finger searches someone out and gives information on that person. The word *finger* refers to both the protocol itself and the software program that runs it. Your basic finger call is done on a particular user (e.g., joeschmoe@wherever.com), and returns such information as whether the user is logged in, when he or she last checked the mail, and a customizable, signature-like file called a plan. Its power can extend to letting someone retrieve a list of all users at a site.

flame

Flame refers to any message that addresses another in a derogatory or attacking way, particularly if, instead of addressing the issue at hand, it attacks the recipient as stupid for having such a point of view in the first place.

frame

Frames are a technology introduced in Netscape 2.0 that allows Web weavers to break the browser window into several smaller windows, each of which can load different things. This means Web masters can create navigation bars and ads that stay with you as you click through a site.

freeware

Freeware is software whose author lets anyone use it freely, without paying for it. Freeware differs from "public-domain" software in that while both are free of charge, a freeware program's author retains the copyright. In other words, you're not allowed to alter the code, incorporate it into software you've written, or pass it off as your own, whether for profit or not. Freeware authors make their software available for the good of the computing community.

FTP

File Transfer Protocol is a program used to find and retrieve software to your computer by downloading it. If you had software you wanted to send to another computer, you'd reverse the process; this is called uploading.

G

GIF

Most of the graphics you run across on the Web will be in the GIF format, a file-type that is readable by most graphics programs. You can tell a file is a GIF by looking at its extension. If its name is something like "file-name.gif," it is a GIF.

GIF animation

Most of the still pictures you will see online are GIFs. However, the latest version of the GIF format allows you to create simple animation in addition to stills. If you browser supports the GIF89a format, you will see animation of figures.

Gopher

Gopher, a precursor to the Web, is a protocol for storing, organizing, and retrieving information on the Internet. Developed at the University of Minnesota, home of the "Golden Gophers," Gopher allows you to navigate up and down through menus to access files. Once you find what you're looking for, Gopher can either download the file for you or display the text. Before the advent of the Web, Gopher was the cutting edge in worldwide information retrieval, allowing you to navigate without typing in complex FTP commands, allowing you actually to browse rather than choose a single destination. Gopher is usually used in one of three ways: from a UNIX shell account, using a Gopher client over a TCP/IP connection, or through a Web browser. Gophers are less and less common these days, however, as most people find Web pages easier to maintain than Gopher servers.

H

hacker

There are two competing definitions of *hacker* floating around. The first is the computer user who knows the technology backwards and forwards, who can see new ways around tough problems, and who creates amazing innovations. The other is the equally knowledgeable person who used his or her expertise to break into elaborate systems for the pride and sheer anarchy of it.

helper app

Your browser can display a wide range of goodies: GIFs, JPEGs, text, even some sound and video. However, sometimes your browser needs help. *Helper app* is used to describe any program that's not a browser per se, but that lets you make use of files that your browser doesn't recognize on its own (such as animation, multimedia, or other specialized resources). When your browser runs across a file it can't understand, it consults its list of helper apps and decides which application it needs to use the file. Helper apps are very similar to plug-ins. Plug-ins also help you deal with strange file types, except plug-ins work within your browser, while helper apps work independently of your browser. That means plug-ins display the information directly in your browser window, while helper apps make their own window.

hits

Web keepers have a difficult time counting how many people come to visit their Web pages. One of the earliest ways of estimating how much "traffic" a site was getting was to count the number of "hits" it got. A hit is a request to the Web server to send along a file.

HTML

HTML (Hypertext Markup Language) is the language used to create hypertext, which means it's the foundation of the Web as we know it. In fact, HTML was used to create every single page you've ever visited on the Web. HTML uses a series of commands written in ASCII text to tell your browser how to display each page, whether it means using a different size, or style, or to display graphics, and create links. If you want to see what the HTML code looks like for whatever page you're on, just use the "View Document Source" command under the "View" menu in your browser.

hypertext

Every Web page that lets you click to go to another Web page, and every page that includes a graphic or other fancy thing, is said to be hypertext. That means that although it appear to you as just one Web page, it's actually composed of several pieces that can be scattered all across the Web.

I

interactive

Interactive refers to any technology that allows the user to exchange information with a computer program, so that the user and the program "interact."

interface

The interface is what you see when you look at your monitor—the collection of words, pictures, buttons, menus, and other things. Every computer program you use has an interface; some are better and some are worse. Graphical interfaces of the Mac and Windows systems affect the interfaces of individual programs. The point of connection between any two parts of the computer (modem and main computer, keyboard, and mouse) is an interface.

Internet

The Internet is a large number of computers that are hooked up to one another all over the world so they can exchange information. To exchange information they use protocols such as FTP, Gopher, and Hypertext Transport Protocol or HTTP.

InterNIC

The Internet Network Information Center (or InterNIC), a private company funded in part by the National Science Foundation, keeps tabs on all registered domains—whether or not the domains are currently in use—and handles registration for newcomers.

IP

Internet Protocol (or IP) is the pack-switching protocol through which everything happens on the Internet. More specifically, it's the underlying network beneath TCP/IP that creates the addressing scheme that allows computers to find each other.

IP address

Just as postal addresses have been codified so that mail can be delivered correctly—name on the first line, company name on the second line, street address third, etc.—IP addresses have been codified to allow Internet information to be delivered correctly. To the Internet, a given server's IP address is all numbers and dots in the formal "000.000.000.0" followed by the word code.

IRC

Internet Relay Chat (or IRC) is the Internet's version of CB radio, a real-time chat network where users can join myriad ongoing discussions. Users connect to an IRC server, which houses many conversations or channels.

ISDN

Integrated Service Digital Network or ISDN is the digital telephone system that has been touted as the replacement for the current slow and noisy analog phone lines. ISDN promises to standardize the high-speed (up to 128 Kbps) transmission of voice, data, and graphic images.

J

java

Java is a computer language that lets programmers create programs that will work for everyone, Mac and PC. Such a program could be as simple as a "stock ticker" that lets information scroll across a Web page, or as complex as an entire game.

JPEG

While GIF is still the dominant graphics format on the Web, JPEG (Joint Photographic Experts Group) is gaining ground fast. Many browsers (including Netscape) now can read JPEGs, and Web page designers have started using the format extensively. The advantage of JPEG is that it uses compression to make graphics files smaller (which means you spend less time waiting for them to load). However, there is some image quality lost to the compression.

K

Kbps

This stands for Kilobits Per Second. It is a measure of throughput and is most often used in association with measuring modem speed. Kilobits per Second should not be confused with Kilo**bytes** per Second. Since there are 8 bits in a byte, a modem that goes at 28.8 Kbps is capable of transmitting only about 3.5K per second.

kermit

An ancient modem protocol used with shell accounts to upload and download files. Similar to X-, Y-, and ZMODEM.

keyword

On the Internet, you use a keyword when you're searching for something. If you were searching for the literary works of Edgar Allen Poe, for example, you would probably search on "Poe," rather than "literary works of Edgar Allen Poe." Many Web designers build keywords into their pages so that search engines can tell what the topics of their pages are.

L

link

Links are the connections between hypertext pages. Every time you click on highlighted text to go to another page on the Web, you're following a link.

lurker

A lurker is anyone who reads the postings in a chat room, IRC channel, Internet newsgroup, or any other electronic place for posting messages but rarely posts messages of his or her own.

listserv

A listserv is a software program that helps a group of users converse via an electronic mailing list, or mail list, that is devoted to a specific topic. People sharing an interest may "subscribe" to a given discussion, and other subscribers' contributions to the thread are distributed to the entire subscriber base via e-mail. When mail is sent to the list from a particular user, it is sent out to all subscribers on the list, thus furthering the conversation.

M

macro

A macro is a handy way to get your computer to do automatically a series of tasks that you would otherwise have to do step by step. For instance, if you send out holiday form letters, you could create a macro that would tell your word-processing software to grab all the addresses from one file and merge them into your letter one by one, creating a personalized effect without your having to cut and paste.

mailing list

Many interest groups have formed mailing lists to keep in touch with each other and exchange their thoughts via e-mail.

mail server

A mail server is the part of your ISP's server that handles incoming and outgoing mail. Every piece of mail you get and send is either fielded or sent on its way by the mail server.

MIME

MIME stands for Multipurpose Internet Mail Extension, and it refers to an extension of traditional text-based Internet e-mail. MIME allows you to send nontextual data, such as audio clips, graphic images, and even faxes, as specially encoded attachments to e-mail messages.

mirror

If a site is mirrored there is "more of" that site. Instead of the Internet just finding that info at Point A, it can find it at either Point A or Point B. This is good for Web users when a site is so popular that it's hard to get through the crowds at Point A.

modem

A modem is a piece of computer equipment that hooks into your phone jack and changes the kinds of electrical signals your computer can work with into the kind of signals that can be passed over the phone lines (analog signals). The modem is also in charge of negotiating connections to other computers.

Mosaic

Mosaic is the Web browser that was the foundation that brought the Web to the masses. Mosaic, developed by the National Center for Supercomputing Applications, was the first Web browser that allowed you to display in-line graphics (showing pictures in the browser). Since then, browsers have added video and sound.

MPEG

MPEG is a popular standard for compressing and playing back full-motion video and audio streams at 30 frames per second on a computer. MPEG format files are commonly found on CD-ROM disks, not to mention Web sites. MPEG stands for Motion Picture Experts Group.

MUD

Multiple User Dungeons are simulated environments that allow users to interact with one another in real time.

N

NCSA

The National Center for Supercomputing Applications (NCSA) is best known to Web surfers as the developer of NCSA Mosaic, the first graphical World Wide Web browser. NCSA is a scientific research center that takes on computing challenges in the interest of science, engineering, education, and business.

negotiation

The racket your modem makes when you go online is negotiation. Your modem is talking with the modem at the other end of the line, figuring out how fast each modem can go and how it wants to handle those bits and bytes. Once they've figured that out, your modem is ready to move the information going to and from the Internet.

netiquette

Netiquette is a combination of the words *network* and *etiquette*. This informal code of manners governs online conduct.

Netscape

Netscape is the leader in Web Browser software with its Netscape Navigator (in version 3). Netscape Communications Corp., as it is formally known, came into being in April 1994 through the efforts of Jim Clark, former chairman of Silicon Graphics, and Marc Anderson, the development brains behind the NCSA Mosaic browser.

network

A network is any connection of two or more computers made for the purpose of sharing resources. These resources could be information, software, or equipment. Networks come in various form, local area networks (LANs), wide area networks (WANs), intranets, internets, and extranets.

newsgroup

Several lively discussions, called newsgroups, are carried on Usenet on several topics. Several conversations, called "threads," are usually going on at once in any group. Usenet is easily reachable through the Net and through your Web browser.

newsreader

A newsreader is a piece of software that lets you read Usenet discussions. Most newsreaders let you subscribe to one or more news groups, select and read others' postings, and post your own comments.

news server

A news server is the computer at your ISP that runs the necessary software that gathers newsgroup information and distributes it to the ISP's subscribers. Your newsreader software, which runs on your PC, gets all its information from the news server.

O

offline reader

An offline reader lets you log on, log off, and then read what you want. Most work like this: When you go online and you may find information you'd like to have your reader check on for you; the next time you're ready to look at those Web pages, the offline reader will fetch them. Once it logs itself off, you can read the pages without racking up phone bills— and since the pages are now stored on your hard drive instead of somewhere on the Net, they load into the browser fast.

online

Being online means being connected to another computer, presumably via phone line. When you log onto your ISP for Internet access, you are online. When you log onto AOL you are also online. A computer that is active on a network can also be said to be online. Another meaning is the status of an Internet server: When online, its network connection is live, and authorized users can access its resources. A printer can also be online; in this instance, it will accept data from its host computer.

operating system

An operating system is what gives your computer its personality and patterns of behavior. There are several kinds of operating systems: MacOS; the DOS-based Windows system, or Unix. One of the toughest challenges computer programmers face is making their programs "cross-platform" or understandable to more than one operating system.

P

packet

This is the smallest unit of information that travels across a network, from the smallest peer-to-peer hookup to the Internet itself. Information to be sent over the Internet is first broken up into packets, all of which are sent independently to the remote computer where they are reassembled.

parity

Parity is a form of error-checking whereby two computers—one sending, another receiving—match the data one sent with what the other received. In your communication software, you set the parity according to what your carrier expects: "no parity" or "even parity." Frequently, a nondata parity bit is attached to each character sent, and the computers at each end of the connection must agree over the parity bit's value, 0 or 1. If the parity bit doesn't match, they know something didn't make it through intact.

PGP

Pretty Good Privacy, or PGP, a program that uses public key encryption to protect files and e-mail. You can also use it to attach a digital signature to a document or message so that people can verify that you were the sender.

ping

Ping is a program that tests communication to and from a network destination such as a connected node. When the computer running the program pings another, it sends a special echo request, waits for an answer, and then sends different-sized packets to measure response time, not to mention watching whether or not the packets even make the trip.

pixel

A pixel is the smallest discernible part of your computer's display—the dots of a monitor's dot-per-inch (dpi) rating (as in 800 x 600 dpi), which is actually measured in pixels.

plug-in

You can expand the capability of your browser by "plugging in" various tools that let you see and hear audio or video files. When your browser needs a plug-in you don't have yet, it will tell you it has encountered an "unknown file type." If the Web page designer is kind, he or she will tell you which plug-in you need and where to get it. Some of the most popular plug-ins are Shockwave, RealAudio, and MPEGplay.

POP

POP has two definitions. The first is "Point of Presence," meant to denote whatever place an Internet service provider keeps the entanglement of computers, router, modems, leased lines, and other equipment it needs to serve its subscriber base and maintain its existence as an Internet site. The second meaning, Post Office Protocol, is used by an ISP's mail server to manage e-mail for subscribers. Another word for an e-mail account is a POP-mail account.

port

Ports are plugs on the back of your computer where you connect peripherals such as printers or modems. Port is also the verb that means modifying a piece of software so it will run on another platform. Windows software, for instance, might be ported to the Mac platform. An Internet port, however, is a part of a server that handles certain kinds of requests. If you've ever seen a number appended to the end of a URL, followed by a colon, that's the port number.

post

The word *post* refers to communications on electronic bulletin boards and newsgroups. It can be used as both a noun and a verb. In an electronic message board or newsgroup, when you upload a message relating to a given thread, you're posting.

postmaster

The postmaster for a given site takes care of the server's mail functions and handles questions and complaints. You can contact someone at a given site by addressing it to postmaster@wherever.com.

PPP

PPP stands for Point-to-Point Protocol. It is one of two common protocols your Internet service provider (ISP) may offer as your way of gaining access to the Internet. PPP, the newer protocol, loads on top of other software called a TCP/IP stack and lets you use your browser instead of the terminal-emulation software Internet users previously used.

Q

query string

A query string is an instruction given to a server by your browser; it's tacked onto the end of a URL. If you do a search on Yahoo, you'll see that the URL that is returned has a question mark in it. Everything after the question mark is the query string.

QuickTime

QuickTime is a video protocol developed by Apple Computer. It has become one of the two main video standards on the Internet and in computers in general. QuickTime is built into MacOS. If you have Windows, you can view QuickTime movies by downloading the QuickTime for Windows plug-in.

R

RBOC

RBOC stands for Regional Bell Operating Company and refers to your local phone company. The RBOCs were created as a result of the breakup of AT&T's monopoly.

remote login

Using the right protocol, you can log in from outside the physical site of a network and access all the resources as if you were on-site.

RJ-11

RJ-11 is the name for the modular connector your telephone and/or modem uses to connect with the telephone wiring of your home and/or office. Before RJ-11 connectors, hooking up a phone meant stripping wires, unscrewing the phone-jack box, and connecting a spaghetti-like mess of multicolored wires to the correct places.

root

Root came from UNIX. It means the topmost directory from which all others branch out. Another UNIX meaning of root is the system administrator's account that has access privileges to everything on the server.

router

This is a hardware device that acts as a gateway between two or more networks. Routers, which are actually types of computers, are designed to comprehend the various protocols the respective networks use—a LAN may run on Ethernet while the Internet runs on TCP/IP—and to translate as necessary to route packets back and forth between the networks.

S

server

A server is a fancy name for a computer that's hooked up to a network (such as your office LAN, or the Internet) or a piece of software that helps that computer do its job. Servers send files across the network where your computer (the client) receives and interprets them.

service provider

An Internet service provider or ISP is a company that provides the gateway between you and the Internet. Online services such as America Online and CompuServe are also touting their ability to provide Internet access. When you use AOL as a launching pad, that service is acting as your ISP. Other ISPs have direct Internet access only.

session

A session includes whatever one does while online from connect time to hang-up, whether transmission, real-time chats, or research.

shareware

Shareware is software that you can download for free, install, and use for a pre-agreed time period. Once the time is up, if you like it, you pay a registration fee. If you do not like it, you delete it.

shell

Shell is the name for the interface that renders the intricacies of an operating system, such as UNIX or DOS, relatively palatable to users. ISPs offer "shell-account" subscribers a shell—Bourne, C, and Korn are examples—that provides the system prompt most people think of when they think UNIX.

shell account

An ISP shell account, intended primarily for diehards and tech-heads, offers subscribers one of the many UNIX shells through which these users enter commands to access services such as Usenet and FTP.

shocked

Shockwave is a tool from a company called Macro Media. Shockwave lets Web creators show a variety of graphics online, such as animations. If you have the right plug-in, anyone can view the animation.

.sig

This is the equivalent of a signature. Uploaders of e-mail or news group message often create signatures out of ASCII characters and occasionally graphics. Once you create and store this digital signature, it's appended to the end of every e-mail message you send.

SMTP

Using POP—the Post Office Protocol—your e-mail program running on your PC talks to any servers that store mail addressed to you. When one server storing mail needs to talk to another, however—to send, receive, or forward mail between servers—it doesn't use POP but its server-to-server equivalent, Simple Mail Transfer Protocol.

socket

A server sits and waits for calls on a given port number. When a client finally does connect with the server, the server devotes that port number to the client and binds what is called a socket—a confirmed end of a two-way connection—to communicate with the client.

source

The source of the document is the HTML code that makes it look the way it looks. The see the source of the page you're on, go to the "View" menu on your browser and select "Document Source" (if you are using Netscape) or "Source" (if you are using Explorer).

spam

The newsgroup and e-mail boxes of the world have already developed their equivalent of junk mail. It's called "spam." When you see the same make-money-fast message in all the newsgroups and in your mailbox, the Net has been spammed.

spider

A spider is a small piece of software that crawls around the Web picking up URLs and information about the pages they represent. Spiders tend to pick up information that is sometimes useful in a search and sometimes not.

stack (TCP/IP)

The TCP/IP stack is a set of software tools that lets your PC communicate using TCP/IP, the standard protocol of the Internet.

sysadmin/sysop

System administrators and system operators do most of the grunt work. In some networks, such as online services, the sysop is instead the referee who steps in when someone has cross-posted a message inappropriately. The sysop moves the message to its proper place and/or notifies the offender.

T

T1/T3

The big-time phone lines leased by big companies, universities, and the government for high-speed Net access and large-scale phone service are called T1s or T3s, depending on the individual line's capacity. T1 lines carry data at a maximum 1,544 Mbps. T1s will still drop frames if you're trying out full-screen, full-motion teleconferencing. T3 lines, on the other hand, are faster than T1s and will accommodate full-screen video.

talk

Talk is a UNIX protocol that lets two people conduct a real-time, text-based conversation over the Internet. You can initiate the conversation by using the command "talk" followed by the e-mail address of the person with whom you wish to speak at the UNIX command line. If that person is online, instructions pop up on the screen of that user, who can return contact and initiate the conversation. This form of talk uses a split screen; one person's typed words appear on the top half, the other's on the bottom.

TCP/IP

TCP/IP is the basic language by which all Internet computers talk to each other and send the tiny chunks of information that make up a Web page. For a service like AOL, there is no need to worry about TCP/IP, but for other users, TCP/IP must be configured.

telnet

Telnet is a way by which you can log into a computer that you're not sitting in front of. For example, you may have an Internet account at your home.com, but you're out of town and your home.com is a long-distance call away. If your home.com allows people with accounts to log in via telnet, you could get onto another computer on the Net and telnet to your home.com computers and check your mail.

terminal emulator

A terminal emulator is any software that, when you run it on a PC, makes the PC resemble a mainframe dumb terminal. "Dumb" refers to their inability to process anything; they only provide a gateway to use the mainframe's processing muscle.

thread

A thread is a multipart virtual conversation on a given topic. Threads can exist in Usenet newsgroups, in the forums of an online service, or in the form of a series of e-mails.

throughput

Throughput is another word for "communications speed." If you uploaded a megabyte in 10 minutes, the throughput would have been 13,981 bits per second—close to the best-case throughput of a 14.4 Kpbs modem, but relatively slow by modern standards.

time out

When you dial into your ISP, your communications software is programmed to wait a certain number of seconds for a response after the line is picked up. If you ISP does not respond in time and initiate the modem's "handshake," your computer hangs up.

U

Unix

Unix was the first operating system that could be used on many different types of computers. Because of this flexibility, people started using it around the world and later used it to handle their Internet needs. The Net and Web grew up on Unix, and many of the computers on the Net still use it for their servers.

upload

Uploading is sending something to another computer.

URL

The URL (Uniform Resource Locator) is the address of a Web page. The first part of the URL (http) tells the browser it's looking for a Web page. The rest gives the name of the computer that holds the page (www.zdnet.com).

uuencoding

Uuencoding allows you to send binary, nontextual files in ASCII format. Uuencoding is most often used for sending binary files via e-mail, or for posting them to a newsgroup. Uuencoding a file should not be confused with compressing it, as uuencoded files typically take up more space than the originals. If you receive a uuencoded file, you need a uudecoding program to make sense of it.

V

veronica

Veronica is a database of Gopher-server menu items. You can search by keywords, a convenient alternative to searching server by server.

virus

A virus is a program that can hide in any disk or software. Viruses can travel across any means of connecting computers, like modems and networks. It may damage the hard disk or corrupt the activities of your operating system. Some viruses can change with every replication from computer to computer. A program like Disinfectant can help to prevent a virus from corrupting your system.

VRML

VRML is a way by which programmers can design and create 3-D places on the Web. Using VRML, a programmer can design a room or a landscape through which you can move and look at things much as you do in the world outside your computer.

W

World Wide Web

Also called WWW, W3, or just the Web, the World Wide Web is the whole gamut of hypertext servers that let HTML programmers present virtual, on-screen pages combining text, graphics, audio, and other file types, as well as links to other pages.

X, Y, Z

xmodem/ymodem/zmodem

Three ancient protocols you can use to transfer files using a PC. XMODEM sends data in 128k blocks and uses one-byte control sequences. YMODEM, an extension to XMODEM, uses better error checking and sends 1K blocks. ZMODEM, the most popular of them all, is also the most reliable, with features such as auto restart of aborted or interrupted transmissions.

References

Ashton, P. T., & Webb, R. B. (1986). *Making a difference: Teacher sense of efficacy and student achievement.* New York: Longman.

Daggett, W. (1998, July). *Collaborating for academic excellence* (Address at School-to-Work Conference, School-to-Career Academy, ASCA, Burlingame, CA). (Available from ASCA, 1575 Bayshore Highway, Burlingame, CA 94010)

Dembo, M. H., & Gibson, S. (1985). Teachers' sense of efficacy: An important factor in school improvement. *The Elementary School Journal, 86*(2), 174-184.

Deming, W. E. (1982). *Out of the crisis.* Cambridge: MIT Press.

Erickson, L. H. (1995). *Stirring the head, heart, and soul: Redefining curriculum and instruction.* Thousand Oaks, CA: Corwin.

Erickson, L. H. (1998). *Concept-based curriculum and instruction* Thousand Oaks, CA: Corwin.

Fullan, M. (1982). *The meaning of educational change.* New York: Teachers College Press.

Glasser, W. M. D. (1990). *The quality school.* New York: HarperCollins.

Goodlad, J. I. (1984). *A place called school.* New York: McGraw-Hill.

Lanier, J. E., & Little, J. W. (1986). Research on teacher education. In M. C. Wittrock (Ed.), *Handbook of research on teaching* (3rd ed.; pp. 527-569). New York: Macmillan.

Little, J. (1982). Norms of collegiality and experimentation: Workplace conditions of school success. *American Educational Research Journal, 19*(Fall), 325-340.

Lortie, D. C. (1975). *School teacher: A sociological study.* Chicago: University of Chicago Press.

Mager, R. (1975). *Instructional objectives.* Belmont, CA: Fearson.

Martin, O. L. (1990). *Instructional leadership behaviors that empower teacher effectiveness.* Paper presented at the annual meeting of the Mid-South Educational Research Association, New Orleans.

Marzano, R. J., & Kendall, J. S. (1996). *A comprehensive guide to designing standards-based districts, schools, and classrooms.* Alexandria, VA: ASCD.

Newmann, F. M., Rutter, R. A., & Smith, M. S. (1989). Organizational factors that affect school sense of efficacy, community, and expectations. *Sociology of Education, 62,* 221-238.

Reksten, L. E. (1995). *Teacher efficacy and the school context.* UMI dissertation Services, Ann Arbor, MI, 1995.

Rosenholtz, S. (1985, May). Effective schools: Interpreting the evidence. *American Journal of Education,* pp. 352-388.

Rosenholtz, S. (1986). Organizational conditions of teacher learning. *Teaching and Teacher Education, 2*(2), 91-104.

Rosenholtz, S. (1987, August). Education reform strategies: Will they increase teacher commitment? *American Journal of Education*, pp. 534-562.

Rosenholtz, S. (1989). *Teachers' workplace: The social organization of schools.* New York: Longman.

Tye, K. A., & Tye, B. B. (1983). *Teaching isolation and school reform. Phi Delta Kappan, 65,* 319-322.

Wenglinsky, H. (1998). *Does it compute? The relationship between educational technology and student achievement in mathematics* (ETS Policy Information Report, September). Princeton, NJ: Educational Testing Service.

Wolfe, P. (1998). *Brain research and implications for education.* (Address given November 9, 1998, at the Autry Museum of Western Heritage, Los Angeles). (Available from Patricia Wolfe, Ed.D., 555 Randolph Street, Napa, CA 94559)

Printed in the United States
86896LV00012B/13-18/A

9 780803 968141